The SEA

Stories, Trivia, Crafts, and Recipes Inspired by the World's Best Shorelines, Beaches, and Oceans

ISOBEL CARLSON

Skyhorse Publishing

Skyhorse Publishing books may be purchased in bulk at special discounts for sales promotion, corporate gifts, fund-raising, or educational purposes. Special editions can also be created to specifications. For details, contact the Special Sales Department, Skyhorse Publishing, 307 West 36th Street, 11th Floor, New York, NY 10018 or info@skyhorsepublishing.com.

Skyhorse® and Skyhorse Publishing® are registered trademarks of Skyhorse Publishing, Inc.®, a Delaware corporation.

Visit our website at www.skyhorsepublishing.com.

10 9 8 7 6 5 4 3 2 1

Library of Congress Cataloging-in-Publication Data is available on file.

Cover design by Summersdale Ltd./Qualcom

Front cover – top left photo (dolphin) – © Willyam Bradberry/Shutterstock.com; top right photo (waves) – © Pavel Vakhrushev/Shutterstock.com; bottom left image (lighthouse) – © LAATA9/Shutterstock.com; bottom middle photo (shells) – © givaga/Shutterstock.com; rope pattern – © Irina Danyliuk/Shutterstock.com

Text by Debbie Chapman
Research by Lizzie Price

Print ISBN: 978-1-5107-4299-4
Ebook ISBN: 978-1-5107-4300-7

Printed in China

For Laura Marmolejo
Who is content, capable, and above all, relevant
And who loves the sea.

CONTENTS

Introduction

There's no doubt about it: a good lungful of seaside air or a quick dip in the sea can work wonders for our health and well-being. For adults and children alike, the ocean is the world's biggest and most mesmerizing playground, delivering a wealth of sensory experiences and providing spiritual sanctuary. And our coastlines offer so much more than sand and sea; they are a treasure trove of spectacular terrains and ever-changing views, and a place for bracing walks, shoreline exploration, exhilarating water sports, and cozy campfires. The sea is also our main resource and home to the most extraordinary collection of living things, from the tiniest zooplankton right up to the gargantuan blue whale.

This book will not only introduce you to some of these beguiling creatures and spellbinding coastlines, but it also includes ideas for seaside activities and recipes to make the most of your time by the sea, as well as crafts that will bring the beach into your home. It will tell you the stories and legends of the deep oceans, fill your mind with fascinating trivia, and give you a good dose of wanderlust.

If this book has one message, it is simply this: go to the sea. Walk along the beach. Breathe in the fresh, salty air, feel the sand between your toes, listen to the crashing waves and the crunching of rocks underfoot. Hear the gulls caw and watch the swooping flight of cormorants and frigatebirds. Catch a wave on a surfboard or dive down to a world of coral reefs and underwater treasures. Collect seaweed and fresh seafood from the shore and cook it on the beach, or hunt for jagged sharks' teeth and fossils among the shingle. Appreciate this immense world for all its weird and wonderful life, protect it where you can, and most of all: enjoy.

The sea is emotion incarnate.
It loves, hates, and weeps. It defies all
attempts to capture it with words.

CHRISTOPHER PAOLINI

The sea is as near as we come to another world.

ANNE STEVENSON

THE SCIENCE OF THE SEA:
Essential Sea Facts

The Basics

- **AREA:** The ocean accounts for almost 71 percent of the Earth's surface.

- **WATER:** Nearly 98 percent of all the water on the planet is found in its oceans.

- **AVERAGE DEPTH:** 2.5 miles (4 kilometers).

- **DEEPEST POINT:** 6.8 miles (11 kilometers): the Pacific Ocean's Mariana Trench; 1 mile (1.6 kilometers) deeper than Mount Everest's height.

- **AVERAGE SURFACE SEA TEMPERATURE:** 62°F (17°C).

- **WATER PRESSURE:** 8 tons per square inch (1.1 tonnes per square centimeter) at the deepest point in the ocean (the equivalent of having 50 jumbo jets on top of you).

- **SALTINESS:** The sea is roughly 96.5 percent water and 3.5 percent salts (including but not limited to sodium chloride, a.k.a. sea salt).

- **COLOR:** Everything in the sea looks blue because the water absorbs all the other colors of sunlight—red, orange, and yellow are absorbed first, then green and violet, until there is only blue light left to reflect.

SEA FACTS TO BLOW YOUR MIND

- Humans have explored less than 10 percent of the world's oceans. We have more detailed maps of the surface of Mars than of the Earth's oceans.

- While the oceans account for 99 percent of the inhabited space on Earth, more than 90 percent of this living space is located in the deep sea.

- Twelve people have set foot on the moon. Just three people have been to the Mariana Trench.

- The Pacific Ocean alone covers more than a third of the Earth's surface and stretches nearly halfway around the world at its widest point. The distance at this point is five times more than the diameter of the moon.

- The speed of sound is faster underwater—nearly four times as fast as the speed of sound in air.

- Photosynthesis in the oceans (from seaweed, seagrass, and phytoplankton) accounts for up to 85 percent of the oxygen in the air we breathe.

- The krill (tiny crustaceans that are an important food source for many marine animals) in the Southern Ocean weigh more than the total weight of the Earth's entire human population.

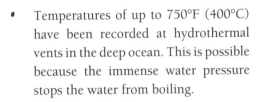

- Temperatures of up to 750°F (400°C) have been recorded at hydrothermal vents in the deep ocean. This is possible because the immense water pressure stops the water from boiling.

- The ice sheet that forms over the ocean in Antarctica every year measures twice the size of the United States.

- The Mediterranean Sea was a dry basin until around five million years ago, when the Atlantic Ocean burst through the Strait of Gibraltar. It only took about two years for the water to fill it in to roughly the shape it is today, pouring into the basin 1,000 times faster than the speed at which the Amazon flows.

- There is marine limestone on the summit of Mount Everest. The Himalayas came into being when the sediments that had formed the bottom of the Tethys Sea (between the Indian subcontinent and Asia) 400 million years ago were forced upwards at an alarming rate (4 inches [10 centimeters] a year!). The upper layers of Everest now contain the fossils of trilobites and other microorganisms that were deposited in the shallow water of the Tethys.

PEBBLES AND FOSSIL HUNTING

The pleasing crunch of pebbles underfoot is one of the most satisfying elements of a trip to the beach—unless you have the luxury of pure-white sand beaches for miles, of course. Take a closer look and you'll discover that there's so much variety and fascinating detail in the stones and rocks you find at the beach. From the dazzling patterns and colors of shiny oval pebbles to semi-precious stones and fossils, you could start a collection to build into a rockery or garden display, or keep the most interesting ones on the mantelpiece or in a glass vase in the bathroom so that you always have a piece of the beach in your home. (Just check first to see if there are restrictions on how many stones you're allowed to take from your local beach—and beware: some beaches prohibit it completely.)

FOSSIL HUNTING

Fossil hunting can be enjoyed by all ages, and it helps to know where exactly on the beach to look. Here's a quick guide to set you on the right path.

ON THE SHINGLE

The beach itself is rich in fossils, the foreshore being the best place to spot them and the most easily accessible. Carefully sift the shingle on the foreshore with your fingers. Even beaches without seawalls or cliffs can offer up some treasure. The tideline, where seaweed is deposited at low tide, is another good place to sift for fossils and amber.

ON SCREE SLOPES

Rock fragments at the base of cliffs are another rich hunting ground for fossils, but check for warning signs of falling rocks and landslides before you set out. Corals and brachiopods can sometimes be plucked from the limestone, and if you're lucky you might even unEarth prehistoric turtle fossils, bird fossils, and large sharks' teeth among the rocks.

IN CLIFFS

Look along the cliff face after a high tide for fossils that have been exposed by the sea, as they will sometimes poke out of the rocks. However, be careful if you're searching at the base of cliffs; wear a hard hat and check for warning signs about falling rocks. The Isle of Wight in the United Kingdom has some particularly good locations for finding fossils in cliffs, such as at Shanklin and Sandown (Yaverland Beach), where, along with fossilized fish and seashells, even dinosaur bones have been unEarthed. The Jurassic Coast in Dorset is also abundant with fossils, particularly ammonites.

UNDER ROCKS

Sometimes the best fossils are hidden, so don't forget to (carefully) lift rocks and boulders if you think you're in a fossil-rich spot.

THE SEA

The sea! the sea! the open sea!
The blue, the fresh, the ever free!
Without a mark, without a bound,
It runneth the Earth's wide regions round;
It plays with the clouds; it mocks the skies;
Or like a cradled creature lies.

I'm on the sea! I'm on the sea!
I am where I would ever be;
With the blue above, and the blue below,
And silence wheresoe'er I go;
If a storm should come and awake the deep,
What matter? I shall ride and sleep.

I love, O, how I love to ride
On the fierce, foaming, bursting tide,
When every mad wave drowns the moon
Or whistles aloft his tempest tune,
And tells how goeth the world below,
And why the sou'west blasts do blow.

I never was on the dull, tame shore,
But I lov'd the great sea more and more,
And backwards flew to her billowy breast,
Like a bird that seeketh its mother's nest;
And a mother she was, and is, to me;
For I was born on the open sea!
The waves were white, and red the morn,

In the noisy hour when I was born;
And the whale it whistled, the porpoise roll'd,
And the dolphins bared their backs of gold;
And never was heard such an outcry wild
As welcom'd to life the ocean-child!

I've liv'd since then, in calm and strife,
Full fifty summers, a sailor's life,
With wealth to spend and a power to range,
But never have sought nor sighed for change;
And Death, whenever he comes to me,
Shall come on the wild, unbounded sea!

BARRY CORNWALL

THE AMALFI COAST

Where? The Amalfi stretch of coastline sits pretty on the southern edge of the Salerno Gulf, just south of Naples, Italy.

Why should I go? If picture-perfect pastel towns clinging to dramatic forest-covered cliffs that dive into the Mediterranean sum up paradise to you, then look no further than Italy's crown jewel.

What should I do? Visit Positano for its colorful array of shops and bars, and Sorrento for its dramatic clifftop views and wonderful seafood; dive into the pristine turquoise sea from any of the coastline's marvelous beaches; take a boat trip to the island of Capri or to view the Amalfi coast from the water; hike along the cliffs; or sample Italy's top wines in the region's many vineyards.

Don't miss: Conca dei Marini, a less visited but equally beautiful village nestled at the foot of a cliff, with its spectacular Grotta dello Smeraldo—a cave carved into the cliffs by the Tyrrhenian Sea.

Stand-Out Coast

OCEAN ODDITIES

The Monterey Submarine Canyon in California is deeper and larger in volume than the Grand Canyon.

There's an underground "ocean" the size of the Arctic Ocean locked in moisture-containing rocks 400 to 800 miles (644–1,287 kilometers) underneath eastern Asia.

In 1992, a shipping container carrying 29,000 Friendly Floatees rubber ducks (as well as red beavers, blue turtles, and green frogs) was lost in the Pacific Ocean. Ducks washed ashore over 17,000 miles (27,359 kilometers) away for more than 15 years afterward, in places as far afield as Hawaii, Britain, and Australia. Most of the yellow ducks have been bleached to white by the sun.

The sea holds nearly 20 million tons (18 million tonnes) of gold—enough that if it were collected and distributed, everyone on Earth would receive 9 pounds (4 kilograms) of gold! Sadly, this is unlikely to happen as the gold is so dilute that each liter of seawater contains on average just 13 billionths of a gram of gold. Happy mining!

The atolls of the Maldives look like pearlescent smoke rings when viewed from above. They were formed millions of years ago as barrier reefs surrounding island volcanoes in the Indian Ocean, before those volcanoes sank. The reefs grew upwards to retain their position, leaving surreal, ring-shaped atolls dotted around the sea.

THE CREATURES THAT LIVE IN THE OCEANS

There are around 240,000 marine species in the world (everything from seaweed right up to the biggest whales), with thousands of new species being discovered every year—an average of four a day! Some estimates say we have still only identified around 10 percent of all underwater species, meaning there are probably at least two million marine species in total. That's a staggering amount of sea life!

The most recent discoveries include a giant tentacle-less box jellyfish, a stargazing shrimp, a humpback dolphin, and a fish capable of breathing air (though only in part—they won't be walking on land any time soon).

And while we know that our oceans contain colorful fish, bizarre inside-out octopuses, and intimidating sharks with rows of razor-sharp teeth, life in the oceans begins under the microscope. Just one scoop of seawater can contain tens of thousands of zooplankton and phytoplankton (miniature organisms including tiny crustaceans, mollusks, and juvenile fish) that feed on bacteria in the water and constitute an essential part of the underwater ecosystem.

The best way to observe a fish is to become a fish.

JACQUES COUSTEAU

Fish evolved long before the dinosaurs and have been on Earth for more than 450 million years. So far we have identified 25,000 species of fish, but there are probably another 15,000 yet to be identified. Here are some mind-boggling facts about these incredible creatures:

- As fish grow, they don't make new scales but their scales increase in size, leaving growth rings (like in tree trunks) which can tell you their age.

- The oldest known fish was a koi carp named Hanako that lived to the impressive age of 226! Ocean-going fish can live to similar ages—the deepwater rougheye rockfish has been known to reach 205 years.

- Clownfish (anemone fish), like several other animal species, can change sex. All clownfish begin life male, and a school of clownfish will be headed by a dominant fish who has become female. When she dies, the most dominant male changes sex and assumes the top position in the hierarchy. If *Finding Nemo* had been true to life, Nemo's dad, Marlin, should have become Nemo's mother shortly after his original mother was eaten by a barracuda.

- The fastest fish in the ocean is the sailfish, which can swim at up to 68 miles per hour (109 kilometers per hour).

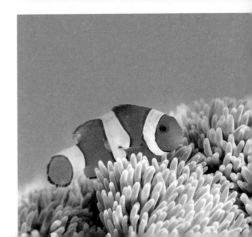

- The longest bony fish alive is the giant oarfish, which can grow up to 36 feet (11 meters) long! It's believed to be the basis for many "giant sea serpent" monster sightings.

- The most abundant creature on Earth is the bristlemouth fish, with thousands of trillions of them around the world—it's millions of times more populous than the world's humans, rats, and chickens combined!

- There are several fish species that have happily lived in the oceans practically unchanged since the time of the dinosaurs. The coelacanth is the oldest species, which is believed to have evolved into its present form 400 million years ago. Sturgeons have existed in their present form for 200 million years (though they face extinction due to overfishing and humans harvesting their eggs for caviar), and the aptly named "dinosaur eels" (which are not eels but fish) have been around since the Cretaceous Period.

- The four-eyed fish has eyes near the top of its head that are split in half horizontally so that it can look both up out of the water and down below the water surface at the same time.

- Jawfish are a family of mouth-breeding fishes, meaning that their eggs hatch in their mouths, where the small fry (young fish) can be protected from predators.

- Flying fish can leap out of the water as a defense mechanism, to escape predators, by propelling themselves into the air at heights of up to 20 feet (6 meters) above the surface with their wing-like fins. The longest known flight time for a flying fish is 45 seconds.

- Stargazer fish have upward-facing mouths and eyes on top of their heads so they can bury themselves in the sand to hide and ambush prey.

- The pufferfish is known for puffing itself into a giant spiky ball when threatened and for being fatal to humans (especially when incorrectly prepared as the Japanese speciality *fugu*), but they have another trick up their sleeves: they use their bodies to create circular patterns in the sand on the sea floor that resemble crop circles—they can be quite intricate and are seemingly an effective way of attracting a mate.

- As far as fish go, seahorses may just be one of the weirdest species. Not only are the males the ones who carry and give birth to their young, but their tails are made up of 36 segments that can pivot, move, and withstand being compressed by 60 percent to avoid being crushed or damaged by prey. Also, they look like tiny sea horses, which is weird enough on its own!

MARITIME HISTORY

Humans have been sailing the seven seas for thousands of years. The oldest known boat in the world is a 10-foot-long (3-meter-long) canoe dating back to c.8000 BCE, which was discovered in the Netherlands, and the earliest known representation of a sailing ship was found in Kuwait and dates back to 5000 BCE, although it has been speculated that *Homo sapiens* first developed seaworthy boats as much as 40,000 years ago. Humans certainly used boats for whaling purposes in prehistoric times by driving whales ashore, and boats or rafts were used in many of the island nations of Polynesia and Asia to get between land masses in ancient times. If you want your mind to be truly blown, picture this: mankind's predecessor, *Homo erectus*, was busy making seaworthy vessels as long ago as 600,000 years before *Homo sapiens* even set foot on the Earth. By the time wood planks were developed to allow humans to build larger ships for war and commerce in around 3000 BCE, boats had been in existence for millennia.

Of course, sailing today is a world away from the early canoes, rafts, and boats. While people still take pride in hand-building their own fishing boats or canoes in many areas around the globe, commercial production of multimillion-dollar superyachts, megayachts, and cruise ships has changed the face of our oceans for ever.

It has also changed the English language, with a multitude of common phrases having their roots in seafaring. If you say something looks "above board," you're invoking the legends of the old pirates who used to menace the seas—they would hide their crews below deck, so honest merchant ships would keep their crew above board to show they were no buccaneers. If the base or "foot" of a sail is not properly connected to the boom, it may become "footloose" (and fancy free). And perhaps most surprisingly, the word *skyscraper* originated from the small, triangular sails set above the main sails, which were so high up they seemed to scrape the sky.

The seven seas are now conventionally given as the Arctic Ocean, the North Atlantic Ocean, the South Atlantic Ocean, the Indian Ocean, the North Pacific Ocean, the South Pacific Ocean, and the Southern Ocean, though perceptions of what constitutes the seven have varied from area to area and throughout history. For example, in medieval Europe, they were given as: the Adriatic Sea, the Mediterranean Sea, the Black Sea, the Caspian Sea, the Persian Gulf, the Arabian Sea, and the Red Sea.

MAURITIUS

Where? The island nation of Mauritius can be found in the Indian Ocean, just east of Madagascar and 1,200 miles (1,931 kilometers) off the east coast of Africa.

Why should I go? Because Mauritius is frequently called Eden or "paradise on Earth," and because you'll never see palm-fringed beaches, waterfalls, and sparkling waters quite like it.

What should I do? What shouldn't you do?! The list of activities you can partake in on the islands is a roll call of all the most fun things to do in life, full stop: kitesurfing, waterskiing, parasailing, swimming with dolphins, zip-lining, quad biking, skydiving, sailing, hiking, horse riding, scuba diving, and snorkeling to see caves, coral reefs, shipwrecks, and fluorescent sea creatures in some of the most crystal-clear waters in the world. You can also take a day trip over to one of the small, uninhabited islands to enjoy pristine beaches and woodland walks in near seclusion, or take a helicopter ride to see the unusual Le Morne "underwater waterfall" illusion.

Don't miss: Mauritius is one of the few places in the world where you can go submarine scootering. These funny-looking devices are one- or two-man pods that enable you to explore the underwater world without requiring diving experience or even being able to swim. You can breathe like normal inside the pod, and you control its movement yourself, giving you free rein to get up close and personal with parrotfish, firefish, bluestripe snappers, butterfly fish, Moorish idols, surgeonfish, and other multicolored beauties swimming around the reef.

Stand-Out Coast

RECIPES:
Fish Dishes

To top off a perfect seaside day, rustle up one of these easy and delicious sea-inspired dishes. Just remember to check that any seafood or fish you buy has been sustainably sourced, and look for line-caught fish wherever possible (see "Protecting Our Oceans: Overfishing" on p.86 for more information).

SEAFOOD PAELLA SERVES 6-8

To taste all the flavors of the sea in one glorious, hot, aromatic dish, nothing beats a classic seafood paella. Experiment with different combinations of seafood, and you could try adding chorizo or chicken if you fancy a more mixed dish. Add a splash of white wine while cooking for an extra twist.

3 tbsp olive oil

1 large onion, finely chopped

4 cloves garlic, finely chopped

1 red pepper, chopped

450 g paella or Arborio rice

1.25 liters chicken stock

Pinch of saffron

2 tsp smoked paprika

1 tsp cayenne pepper

Salt and pepper, to taste

100 g frozen peas

200 g chopped tomatoes

20–24 raw, peeled king prawns

500 g monkfish, cut into chunks,
or 2 squid, cleaned and diced

500 g mussels, cleaned
and de-bearded

Handful of parsley and/
or thyme, chopped

Lemon wedges, to serve

Heat the olive oil in a large pan over a medium heat, then add the onion, garlic, and pepper and cook for 3 minutes. Add the rice and cook for another 2 minutes, stirring continuously, before adding half the stock and the saffron, paprika, cayenne pepper, and seasoning. Bring to the boil and let simmer for 15 minutes, stirring frequently.

Meanwhile, brown the monkfish or squid for a few minutes in olive oil in a separate pan, then set aside.

Slowly add more of the stock to the rice and continue stirring until it's cooked. Add the peas, tomatoes, prawns, monkfish or squid, and mussels, cover the pan with a lid or foil, and cook until the mussels are open. Discard any mussels that remain closed after around 15 minutes.

Sprinkle with parsley and/or thyme and serve with lemon wedges.

SALT-CURED HADDOCK WITH PEAS, POTATOES, AND MINT SERVES 6

This fresh and flavorsome dish is a perfect warmer after those first springtime dips in the sea. It takes a few days to cure the fish, but it's worth doing it yourself for a showstopper of a meal. Source local and fresh ingredients to ensure the most flavor.

To cure your haddock, blend any of the optional extra ingredients in a food processor until you have a fine paste, and mix with the salt. Use a third of the mixture to cover the bottom of a dish (or a large piece of cling film) and place half of your haddock on top. Cover with another third of the mixture, then place the remaining fillets on top of that, ensuring all the raw fish is covered. Finish off with the remaining salt mix and either cover the dish or wrap the cling film round the fillets firmly. Keep in the fridge for 2 days.

When you're ready to prepare the dish, rinse the fillets under cold water and dry with paper towels. Cut the fillets into chunks. Bring a pan of water to the boil and add the fish, lightly poaching for 2 minutes. Remove from the water and leave to one side, topping with a squeeze of fresh lemon.

Cut the new potatoes into cubes and simmer for 6 to 8 minutes or until they begin to soften. Heat the olive oil in a large pan and add the onion, sweating for a few minutes until soft. Add the garlic, cooked potatoes, and peas, and turn up the heat, cooking for 3 minutes. Add a splash of water to prevent sticking and let simmer for 5 minutes. Season well, then add the fish chunks. Keep cooking at a high heat for 2 minutes.

Remove from the heat, zest the lemon over the top, and add the mint. Serve warm.

FOR THE SALT-CURED HADDOCK

1 kg haddock (4 raw haddock fillets)
400 g sea salt or rock salt

OPTIONAL EXTRAS

50 g fennel seeds
Handful of rosemary sprigs
Handful of fresh thyme
Zest of 2 lemons
100 g caster sugar

FOR THE DISH

3 tbsp olive oil
1 onion, finely chopped
2 garlic cloves, finely sliced
10 new potatoes
400 g peas
Salt and pepper, to taste
Handful of fresh mint, chopped
1 lemon

OCEAN CRAFTS: *Driftwood Art* ···

Driftwood is brilliant—bring a chunk of interestingly gnarled driftwood home and put it on the mantelpiece and you have an instant piece of natural art, giving your house immediate seaside vibes. Use small pieces in displays of seashore finds or tied through with string to create decorative garlands for the house or garden. Flat pieces can be painted on to create unusual and bespoke pieces of artwork. Or, follow these quick instructions and you'll have a rustic birdhouse to hang in your garden, so you'll always have a piece of the beach nearby:

The ocean stirs the heart, inspires the imagination, and brings eternal joy to the soul.

ROBERT WYLAND

1. Collect lots of long, narrow strips of driftwood (you can adapt this if you only have larger pieces).

2. Use a saw to cut flat bottoms on the strips and to trim any bumpy edges or bits sticking out along the edge of the piece. If your driftwood is particularly long, you can cut it in half and use the cut edges as the bottoms. You want each piece to be about 8 inches long, with one or two shorter pieces to create the opening. Use sandpaper to smooth any sharp edges around the entry hole.

3. Cut a piece of flat wood into a circle of around 8 inches diameter; this will be your base. Use wood glue or a hot-glue gun to attach each strip of wood around the edges, applying a thin line of glue along the side of the strip to attach it to the next piece. Use small nails through the lower part of the strips through to the base to give extra stability.

4. Depending on the thickness of your wood strips, align the one or two shorter pieces of wood so they create an opening for the birds to get in. Glue offcuts at the top, leaving a hole of around 1 to 2 inches in diameter (depending on the type of bird you want to attract) and check again that there are no sharp edges where the birds will fly in.

5. Work your way around until you have a cylindrical structure of wood strips. Use glue and small nails to attach offcuts and extra pieces of wood at angles to form a roof.

6. Once all the glue is dry, screw in an eye hook along the top, and thread wire or twine through to hang it. Make sure your birdhouse hangs about 5 feet off the ground to keep your new bird friends safe from predators.

SEA LIFE: *SEABIRDS*

There are around 325 species of seabird, spread across practically every corner of the globe. With their webbed feet to help them get around both on land and in water, and their swooping, majestic flight and sudden dives, they're easy to spot and often striking to look at—especially the huge albatross (with a wingspan of up to 11.5 feet [3.5 meters]), the comical-looking puffin, and the stately frigatebird with its hooked bill and pointed tail and wings. They are well adapted to life at sea, with built-in sunglasses to help with the glare from the water and special salt glands to filter the salt from the seawater and fish they consume and excrete it through their nostrils.

Seabirds have inadvertently aided humans for centuries, helping lost sailors find their way back to land or leading fishermen to ripe hunting grounds. Guano from seabird colonies even helps act as fertilizer for fisheries. However, humans haven't always been so kind in return, hunting seabirds for their meat and collecting their eggs for food, as well as capturing birds such as cormorants to use as fish catchers—the birds are tethered to boats and have a snare tied around their throat so they cannot swallow the fish they catch, meaning the fishermen can pull them back to the boat and force them to spit their catch back up.

Seabirds can travel huge distances, with the tiny Arctic tern traveling to Antarctica and back from the northern hemisphere every year (the longest recorded annual migration of an Arctic tern was 59,650 miles [95,997 kilometers]). Other breeds, such as the sooty tern, are known to stay at sea for years without ever touching land, simply picking fish from the surface of the sea and stealing a couple of seconds to nap mid-flight. Frigatebirds have been recorded as staying in flight for up to 185 days, over 34,000 miles (54,717 kilometers), without rest—that's more than the distance of a complete trip around the world.

PENGUINS

Penguins may well be the most beloved of all aquatic birds, and it's not hard to see why. From the smallest—the little blue penguin, at 16 inches (40 centimeters) tall—to the tallest—the emperor penguin, at 4 feet (1.2 meters) tall—they're distinctive and unique, and exhibit many traits that endear them to us humans. For instance:

- It is a well-documented fact that many species of penguin will mate with the same penguin for life (or at least for several seasons).

- The male penguin (in some species) incubates the egg, and both parents share the duty of bringing up their (undeniably cute and fluffy) young.

- They huddle together for warmth in their massive colonies.

- Penguins aren't afraid of humans (because they don't have many predators who would attack them from solid ground) so appear tame and inquisitive.

- They have been known to show behavior that resembles human displays of jealousy and aren't scared to steal from other penguins—whether it's a rock to make sure they have the finest nest around, or even another chick if their own young dies.

Despite all these cute features that may make penguins seem frivolous, they're very efficiently adapted to life in their all-southern-hemisphere habitats, with swimming speeds of up to 22 miles per hour—35 kilometers per hour—(gentoo penguins), diving depths of up to 265 meters—870 feet—(emperor penguins), excellent hearing, and effective camouflage from both sea and sky with their white bellies and black backs.

Sailing

- The fastest sailing speed on record is 65.45 knots—that's more than 75 miles per hour (120 kilometers per hour)—by the *Sailrocket 2* off the coast of Namibia in 2012.

- Sailing has had the longest winning streak across all sports history. The America's Cup is the oldest international sporting trophy and was in the hands of the New York Yacht Club from 1851 to 1983—132 years! The cup is named after the winning yacht in 1851, *America*, not the country. The NYYC reign was brought to an end by the Royal Perth Yacht Club in their yacht, *Australia II*.

- Australian Jessica Watson sailed a boat single-handedly, nonstop and unassisted, around the world at the age of 16.

- Due to the length of time a regatta can take to complete (often over a week), most Olympic sailors can only win one medal per Olympic Games. However, some Olympians have won five Olympic sailing medals over several years: Ben Ainslie of Great Britain has four gold medals and one silver; Robert Scheidt of Brazil has two golds, two silvers, and a bronze; and Torben Grael (also of Brazil) has two golds, a silver, and two bronze medals.

The winds and the waves are always on the side of the ablest navigators.

EDWARD GIBBON

Mind Your Language: Knowing Your Ships from Your Yachts

You don't want to upset sailing types by inadvertently calling their favorite yacht a boat. Use this cheat sheet to give you a rough guide:

A **boat** is any vessel, for pleasure, residential, or commercial use, that floats on water, and it is usually under 200 feet (about 60 meters) from the forwardmost tip of the bow to the aftermost end of the stern. This includes sailing boats, paddleboats, motorboats, kayaks, and canoes.

Anything over 197 feet (60 meters) in length is generally a **ship**. This includes cruise ships, naval ships, container ships, and tankers.

A **yacht** is a medium-sized vessel—usually one that is very elegant and luxurious. In general terms, it is longer than 30 feet (9 meters)—below this length it is a **pleasure boat**—that floats on water and is used for pleasure. (**Chartered yachts** have professional crews and paying customers, so are technically commercial, but their customers are on board the yacht for pleasure.)

Most **yachts** are **boats**, but if they're particularly large (called a **megayacht** or a **superyacht**) they may be **ships**.

COASTLINE FORMATIONS AND FEATURES

The line where the ocean meets the shore can be a smooth transition from seabed to pristine white sand, or it can take on a more dramatic personality—jagged cliffs jutting skywards, elegant peninsulas stretching out as far as the eye can see, or twisting, zigzagging, meandering fjords. They're all formed by ocean waves wearing away at the land, at different speeds and under different conditions—and for every area where rocks are crumbled and swept away, there's another piece of land being built up by the deposited debris. Here's a concise guide to the main coastal features:

> In every out-thrust headland, in every curving beach, in every grain of sand there is the story of the Earth.
>
> RACHEL CARSON

SEA CAVES

When waves attack hard rock at sea level, the erosion takes place slowly and can gradually carve out sea caves at the base of a cliff—although over time most cave ceilings will collapse under their own weight. The stronger the rock, the larger the caves that can form.

CLIFFS

When the sea crashes against high land repeatedly over long periods of time, it erodes the rock at sea level, undercutting the above land, which eventually comes crashing down into the sea. This leaves a sheer drop, sometimes an incredibly high one, known as a cliff.

Stacks

A disintegrating headland will naturally crumble away at its weakest points first, leaving behind stronger, resilient rock that ends up as a stand-alone stack of super-hard rock, jutting out into the sea. These are temporary features in the grand scheme of things, as they will inevitably crumble into the sea in time.

SEA ARCHES

These are formed when waves crash against a headland from both sides. The erosion on both sides carves sea caves, which eventually break through the rock to join up—leaving a natural archway. Though they're fairly rare (the conditions have to be right to avoid the rock just collapsing), some of the world's most dramatic arches have existed for centuries.

Peninsulas

A peninsula has a very similar definition to a headland—a piece of land, connected to the mainland, that juts out to sea and is surrounded on three sides by water—but this term usually refers to much larger land formations. For example, the world's largest peninsula is over 1.25 million square miles (3.2 million square kilometers) in size: the Arabian Peninsula.

BAYS, GULFS, AND COVES

A bay is any recessed body of water that connects to a larger body of water (in this case, the ocean) and is flanked on three sides by land. They are formed when weaker rocks erode faster than the surrounding, more resilient rocks (which form headlands). A large bay is called a gulf and a small bay is called a cove.

ISTHMUSES

An isthmus is a narrow strip of land that connects two other pieces of land—connecting a peninsula to the mainland, for instance. It has water on two sides.

Headlands and capes

On a coastline made up of various types of rock, the softer rock gets worn away first, creating bays but leaving a promontory of hard rock—often high and with sheer edges—sticking out to sea, flanked by water on three sides. Headlands protect the bays from harsh waves, meaning that soft-sand beaches often form in the sheltered bay of a headland. Large headlands are usually called capes.

ISLANDS

There are many ways that islands can be formed, but they are any piece of land that is surrounded entirely by water. Smaller islands are called islets, skerries, cays, keys, or holms.

ARCHIPELAGOS

A group or chain of islands, often volcanic, which are geographically or geologically related. The largest in the world is the Archipelago Sea in Finland, but other well-known archipelagos include Indonesia, the Philippines, Hawaii, and the Maldives.

Fjords

Fjords are long, steep-sided inlets of water that were formed by glaciers carving their way through valleys. Now that the glaciers are gone, we're left with the dramatic, winding, "lovely crinkly edges" (as described by Douglas Adams) that famously make Norway's coast over ten times as long as it would be without them.

Salt marshes

Salt marshes are valuable ecosystems found at the intertidal zone between land and the sea. Because it is regularly flooded by ebbing tides, it is usually dominated by salt-tolerant hardy grasses and shrubs. They not only provide coastal protection, but also help deliver nutrients to the sea and support the marine food web.

Deltas

When rivers reach the sea, they carry mud and sand out with them. This sediment is usually washed away, but if there's enough of it, the sediment can build up into soft, muddy, marshy land that forces the river into an array of small channels, often in impressively intricate shapes. The sediment builds up over time to create firmer land that is incredibly fertile and can support a lot of wildlife.

Beaches

The crumbling cliffs and rocks that have eroded from all of the other types of coastline eventually get deposited in smaller pieces on an area of flat land known as a beach. The size of the smashed-up rocks determines whether a beach is shingle (larger pieces of rock) or sand (fine, small grains of rock and minerals). Beaches are constantly evolving, as sand or pebbles are washed away and replaced by deposits of new material.

Spits

When pebbles, rocks, and sand are swept away from the land and are deposited in a long beach extending out to sea, this is called a spit. They are constantly evolving and can grow at impressive speeds—up to 15 feet (4.5 meters) a year.

Dunes

When sand is swept away from the sea by wind and is deposited further inland, it builds up into what we call dunes. Eventually, plants that grow in the sand spread their roots among the dunes, which makes them more stable.

BEACH WALKS

For those of us who feel a deep affinity with the ocean, there's nothing better than simply having it as a companion at our side on a long seaside stroll. Listen to the infinitely soothing sounds of the crashing waves, the seabirds calling overhead, the chatter of other families enjoying the beach, and the peace and silence a beach can bring when all those things fade away. On wintry days, the brisk sea air refreshes our souls and lifts our moods; in the summer, a walk by the sea is the perfect way to get away from the hustle and bustle of hot, city life, maybe even dipping a toe into the fresh water to cool us down; and a walk on the beach in the moonlight is a glorious moment everyone should experience at least once.

Several coastal towns host nocturnal shoreline rambles (with some even creating fundraising opportunities to make your walk doubly worthwhile)—check with local organizations and tourist information points. Lots of wildlife comes out at night, so on a clear night, look out for owls hunting for mice and voles, seals and dolphins popping their heads above the water, and huge, colorful moths flitting around any sources of light. But, if you're out of luck, you can always spread a blanket on the sand, stretch out, and enjoy the view of the heavens.

Nobody should rely on a lucky star when walking at night, so if you're not going as part of an organized walk, make sure you take a friend, a flashlight, a basic first-aid kit, and a fully charged mobile phone.

Promenading by the Beach

The word *promenade* has many meanings nowadays: it has kept its original French meaning (*promener*, to walk) as well as being applied to the location where the walking itself takes place, and a "prom" is a formal, square, or school dance and also the famous summer series of concerts at the Royal Albert Hall in England (of which the Last Night of the Proms is the most famous). But it is most closely associated with seafront walking—an association that came about in the nineteenth century when visits to seaside resorts became popular and long stretches of wide walkways were created along the coast for people to take the sea air. Also known as an esplanade or boardwalk, the promenade was the place to be seen. If beach walking is your thing, here are some bucket-list promenades to tick off:

☐ Tel Aviv Promenade, Israel

☐ Rambla de Montevideo, Uruguay

☐ Esplanadi, Helsinki, Finland

☐ Valletta Waterfront, Malta

☐ Brighton Pier and Promenade, England

☐ Promenade Beach, Pondicherry, India

☐ Gold Coast Oceanway, Australia

☐ Santa Cruz Beach Boardwalk or Venice

☐ Beach Boardwalk, California, United States

☐ Copacabana Beach Promenade, Rio de Janeiro

☐ Llandudno Promenade, Wales

Stand-Out Coast

ICELAND

Where? The entire coast around this Nordic island is pretty spectacular, but especially Reykjavík, the Snæfellsnes peninsula, Vík, Akureyri, the Westfjords, and the Westman Islands.

Why should I go? If you think you've breathed fresh air and you haven't been to Iceland, you're wrong—experience the crisp, cool air, the dramatic black sand beaches, and the ice caps and volcanoes looming over intricate fjords, where icy waters crash against steep cliffs.

What should I do? Take a tour or hire a car to drive from Reykjavík up and round the magnificent Snæfellsnes peninsula—the inspiration for *Journey to the Center of the Earth*—and on to the wild and rugged Westfjords, which look like they should be the picture definition of the word *adventure*; watch humpback and blue whales and dolphins from Húsavík; witness the Northern Lights (in winter) or the midnight sun (in summer)—both equally miraculous experiences.

Don't miss: Hvítserkur—a craggy, photogenic, marbled, multicolored rock formation jutting

SEA LIFE: CORAL

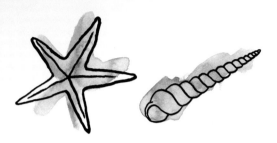

Far from just being a colorful and fascinating addition to any scuba diver's bucket list, or something to admire for their beauty and abundance of bright sea life, coral reefs play a huge part in maintaining the delicate balance of life in the oceans—and they even protect us humans.

There are three types of coral reef: barrier reefs, fringing reefs, and atolls. It is these "barrier" reefs that protect communities living near the sea from wave and storm damage, as well as protecting our shallow waters along the coastline, giving shelter to many types of life along the shore.

A coral is a marine invertebrate, capable of catching fish and plankton but usually relying on photosynthesis for its energy. Coral reefs are thriving communities of living creatures, held together by the calcium carbonate that corals secrete. Though they occupy less than 1 percent of the world's surface, they are home to a quarter of all marine life, including 4,000 different coral reef fish species and many thousands of species of mollusk, crustacean, echinoderm, worm, sponge, sea anemone, jellyfish, and sea squirt. Many sea creatures choose to spawn in them, hiding their eggs in the safety of the reef. Coral reefs can also act as a filter, trapping things that float in the surrounding waters, meaning the quality and cleanliness of the nearby water improves, plus they have their own natural form of sunscreen—protective barriers that let them survive even under the sun's strong rays in the tropical waters where they're found. Pretty impressive!

Of course, the most famous reef of all is the Great Barrier Reef off the coast of Queensland, Australia—and rightly so. It is the largest single structure created by living organisms in the world: it measures 1,300 miles (2,092 kilometers) long over an area of 133,000 square miles (344,468 square kilometers); it consists of over 2,900 individual reefs, 900 islands, and billions of individual living creatures. It can even be seen from the moon.

REEFS IN DANGER

As impressive and magical as coral reefs are, they're in extreme danger—from pollution, bleaching as a result of global warming, and destruction from human activities such as overfishing, destructive fishing methods, harvesting and displacement, coastal development, sedimentation, and irresponsible tourism. Over 60 percent of the world's remaining reefs are at significant risk. Some estimates claim that we have already lost 27 percent of coral reefs worldwide, and that by 2050 there will be only 30 percent left unless action is taken to protect marine habitats (currently less than half a percent of marine habitats are protected) and slow down global warming.

RECIPES:
Picnic Ideas

Is there any finer way to spend a sunny afternoon than with a picnic on the beach? Pack up a picnic blanket or tablecloth, pop some bottles of frozen water (or see the drinks on p.118 for other ideas) and some of the following picnic foods in a cooler, and you're set. Just don't forget the sunscreen!

HERBY POTATO SALAD SERVES 4

The perennial picnic favorite, a fresh and herby potato salad just can't be beaten. Whip this one up the day before and keep it in a sealed container in the fridge, ready to go.

500 g small or fingerling potatoes, chopped
Pinch of salt
1 tbsp olive oil
Large handful of fresh parsley, chopped
1 red onion, diced
Juice of 1 lemon
1 tsp Dijon mustard
1 clove garlic, chopped
Pepper, to taste

Bring a pan of water to boil and add the sliced potatoes and salt. Reduce to a medium simmer and cook for 6 to 8 minutes, until the potatoes are starting to soften. Drain and transfer potatoes to a large bowl.

Blend together the olive oil, half the parsley, half the spring onions, the lemon juice, mustard, garlic, and pepper until they make a paste. Add around ¼ cup of water and blend to combine.

Drizzle the mixture over the potatoes and toss, leaving to one side for 10 minutes for the potatoes to soak up the dressing. Taste and add more salt or pepper to season as necessary, then top with the remaining parsley and onions.

Green Bean and Feta Salad
SERVES 4

700 g fresh green beans
200 g cannellini beans
1 red onion, finely chopped
300 g feta cheese
¾ cup olive oil
⅓ cup white wine vinegar
3 garlic cloves, roughly chopped
Salt and pepper, to taste
Handful of fresh herbs (mint, thyme, basil or your preference)

Optional extras
Seeds or chopped nuts
Tomato, cut into small chunks

This is a delightful, fresh, and summery salad, with the crisp crunch of the beans and the crumbly goodness of the feta cheese.

....

Cut the ends off the green beans and discard, then chop the beans into small pieces. Blanch them in a large pot of boiling water for 3 minutes, then immediately plunge into cold water. Drain well.

Place beans in a bowl and add the red onion, cannellini beans, and feta cheese.

Blend the oil, white wine vinegar, garlic, seasoning, and herbs in a food processor until combined. Pour dressing over salad and toss. Sprinkle with seeds or chopped nuts if you fancy, or for a zesty twist, add tomato chunks.

Potted Shrimp
SERVES 4

For this classic starter, it's best to source pre-cooked and peeled shrimps to save time (250 g is a lot of shrimp!). As they're served cool, you can make this dish in advance (just remove from the fridge 15 minutes before serving). It will keep for up to a week in the fridge.

· ·

Place the butter, lemon juice, cayenne pepper, nutmeg, and anchovy paste into a saucepan and simmer for 2 to 3 minutes. Remove from the heat and allow to cool to room temperature before adding the shrimps to the mixture. Stir well and season to taste. Pack the mixture into individual ramekins and put in the fridge to set. Serve with hot bread.

100 g unsalted butter
Juice of half a lemon
Pinch of cayenne pepper
Pinch of ground nutmeg
1 tsp anchovy paste
250 g cooked and peeled
brown shrimps
Salt and pepper, to taste
Bread to serve—try ciabatta or
Melba toast for an alternative
to traditional brown bread

SURFING, WINDSURFING, AND KITESURFING

Humans have been playing around in the water for millennia, but the art of standing up on what we now call surfboards originated with the ancient Polynesians. In Hawaii, it was called *he'e nalu*, which means "wave sliding," and was an art form they took very seriously, with offerings to the gods whenever they cut wood from the trees to make a new surfboard and intricate rituals surrounding the creation and use of a surfboard.

Though there's evidence that the Polynesians used sails attached to their surfboards thousands of years ago, it wasn't until the latter half of the twentieth century that surfing's sister sports, windsurfing and kitesurfing, were developed as we know them today and first became popular. Whether you've never touched a board before or you're a seasoned wave-rider, here are our top picks for water-sport destinations around the world:

SURFING

Beginner's paradise: There are surf schools dotted around Sri Lanka's spectacular coast, but Weligama or Arugam Bay have the best conditions for beginners, with steady waves, warm seas, and uncrowded beaches.

Bucket-list destination: Bondi Beach, Australia—a place that will forever be synonymous with the chilled-out surfer's lifestyle. The word *Bondi* even means "water breaking over rocks" in the Aboriginal language. Not only are the waves tremendous for surfing, but the beach and surrounding bars and restaurants combine to make the ultimate surfer's paradise.

WINDSURFING

Beginner's paradise: The Greek islands offer perfect windsurfing conditions, and across the 1,400 islands you're sure to find the beach and windsurfing school that's right for you. Kos, Sigri, and Naxos provide beginner lessons and the perfect introduction to windsurfing.

Bucket-list destination: Los Barriles, Baja California—perpetually warm waters, constant sunshine, chilled-out vibes, and stormy waves from November to March mean this should be on every windsurfer's list.

KITESURFING

Beginner's paradise: For calm, warm, and not-too-deep water, with a steady breeze, try one of the kitesurfing schools in the shallow lagoon at Le Morne, Mauritius, before you advance to the nearby beaches with stronger waves.

Bucket-list destination: Kite Beach, Maui—a long, clean, tropical beach, with constant trade winds kicking up some interesting waves for the more experienced rider (especially between October and April).

Other top water-sport destinations:

- ***Hawaii:*** Whether you go to Waikiki, Hanalei Bay, or the North Shore of Oahu, you can't go wrong in the home of surfing
- ***Indonesia:*** Kuta or Uluwatu, Bali
- ***Costa Rica:*** Playa Grande
- ***South Africa:*** Jeffreys Bay
- ***France:*** Biarritz or Hossegor
- ***Portugal:*** Lagos
- ***UK:*** Thurso, Scotland, or Newquay or Croyde, England

SEA LIFE: TURTLES

Think the dinosaurs were pretty ancient? Well, they became extinct 65 million years ago... and turtles have been around for 150 million years. However, of the seven different species of sea turtle, six are now endangered, almost all directly as a result of human behavior, whether it's loss of habitat, entanglement in fishing nets, pollution, global warming, or hunting for consumption or medicine.

These magnificent creatures start their lives on a beach, where a female will lay up to 150 eggs at a time—this beach will be the same nesting ground where the female was born. The sex of the hatchling depends on the temperature of the environment the egg incubates in—warmer temperatures lead to more female turtles, and cooler temperatures lead to more males. Life is treacherous for young hatchlings, as they face immense danger on their journey to the sea and then from the sea itself until their shells harden to give protection from predators—in fact, only 1 hatchling in 1,000 survives into adulthood.

For those that make it, however, they can live extraordinary lives. Sea turtles have an average lifespan of 80 years but have been known to live for well over 100 years—one turtle in an aquarium in China was thought to be over 400 years old, though it's hard to determine a turtle's age for sure. Males will spend their entire lives at sea, whereas females usually go back to shore only to lay their eggs every 2 to 3 years once they've reached maturity—at any age between 10 and 50 years, depending on the species. Leatherback turtles (the largest species) can travel more than 10,000 miles (16,093 kilometers) a year and can weigh up to 2,000 pounds (900 kilograms).

Did You Know?

Sea turtles often look like they're crying, which gives them a very melancholy air. However, they're not sad; they're just using the specialized salt glands behind their eyes to wash away the excess salt they consume from the seawater (it helps flush sand out of their eyes too). So it's practical crying—nothing to shed tears about.

FORAGING

The seashore is the perfect place to gather wild, fresh, and free food for a delicious dinner, especially as there are very few poisonous or inedible species that will cause you harm—that's not to say you shouldn't exercise common sense, though. Follow these top tips for tracking down tasty treats:

1. Look for beaches that have been certified for high standards of cleanliness (your local government or environmental agency websites are the best places to check) so you know that both the beach and the water are clean.

2. According to folklore, you should only collect filter feeders (mollusks, barnacles, and porcelain crabs) in months with an "r" in them (i.e., not May, June, July, or August) to avoid the increased bacteria that can be found in warm waters during high summer.

3. Do not collect anything from the sea during a "red tide," when algae stains the waters red—the potentially harmful blooms of the algae may contaminate your seafood.

4. Make sure you can safely identify the species you're foraging—luckily there aren't too many coastal species that are off limits, but you want to be safe! Invest in a good field guide if you want to become a true foraging expert.

5. Always clean any foraged foods thoroughly before use— wild food is naturally chemical- and pesticide-free, but still might have other nasties on it!

SEA VEGETABLES

There are plenty of delicious coastal plants to add to your diet. Here are just a few to try:

Seaweed

All seaweeds are edible, though not all are to everyone's taste. Look for bladderwrack, wakame, kombu, nori, dulse, Irish moss, and arame for the popular varieties. Most seaweed tastes best when dried and then fried, but if in doubt just treat it like you would spinach, and add it to dishes either raw or lightly wilted or pan-fried with a little butter. You can even make seaweed crisps by coating them in olive oil and salt and roasting them in the oven.

Sea kale

Though this species was once almost foraged to extinction, it's back to healthy levels now, and as long as you don't take too much it's usually fine to forage. Try the leaves fried in oil with a little garlic or sea salt.

Rock samphire

Also known as sea asparagus, this hardy little plant can be found growing all along the high-tide mark and is best picked in spring or summer. Its strong, salty flavor pairs well with mushrooms, fish, and cheese, and they're delicious lightly steamed or boiled and served with butter and black pepper—but avoid the woody stalks.

Other coastal vegetables to look for include: sea radish, sea purslane, sea arrow grass, sea beet, sea blight, watercress, yarrow, glasswort, oyster leaf, buck's horn plantain, sea plantain, sea carrot, chervil, burdock, sorrel, sea buckthorn, and many more! Most of these can be eaten either raw in salads or wilted (especially tasty served in garlic butter), although the fruit of the buckthorn is sweet and makes a wonderful juice.

EDIBLE SHELLFISH

Here are some of the easiest marine animals to try out to get you started:

Whelks, winkles, and cockles

Search for these on rocks or hidden in the sand—sometimes cockles are only spotted by the tiny dimples their shells make in the sand. Before eating any mollusks, you need to clean them thoroughly and then leave them to soak in salted water for at least half an hour (or several hours for larger species).

Mussels

Mussels can be found most easily on rocky shores, but you can also hunt for them on jetties or even on the hulls of boats. Look for shiny, firmly closed mussels and only pick a few from each area—you don't want to eradicate an entire colony. For the best flavor, look for mid-sized mussels. Lots will be easily harvested by simply twisting the mussel and pulling it, but you can come prepared with a pocketknife to cut away the beard on any tough ones. After cooking, discard any that remain closed.

Razor clams

These are tricky to find as they hide deep in the sand, but if you manage to locate some and happen to have salt on hand, sprinkling it over their burrow will force them out into the open where you can catch them. They don't look particularly appetizing but, pan-fried in butter, the scallop-like taste is enough to make the effort worthwhile.

A word about crabs

There are plenty of other edible species to be found on the shore, including plenty of fish, of course. If you're tempted by a crab supper, however, bear in mind that not only do most beaches have local by-laws that prohibit taking home certain species of crab and lobster, but you should also be able to sex the animal (putting all females back to maintain breeding populations), and you'll have to be able to identify the species from each other (not all are edible), *and* you should be able to age the specimen, to make sure you're not putting local populations at risk. Even taking all of that into account, it's worth considering that studies show that crabs and lobsters are incredibly intelligent creatures that can feel pain, can live up to 100 years in the wild, and have complex social networks—plus there's no humane way to kill them. Is your lobster sandwich really worth all that hassle?

THE RULES OF FORAGING:

- Only take what you need and what you will eat.

- Make sure you don't damage any plants or wildlife while foraging.

- Never pull a plant up at its root—if you take just the leaves or fruit of a plant, most species will regrow to be foraged again.

- Make sure you're not trespassing on private land.

- Check for local by-laws that may prohibit the foraging of certain species or in certain areas.

BIG SUR

Where? Big Sur is an expanse of the central coast of California, from San Simeon to Carmel. Bordered by the Pacific Ocean on one side and the Santa Lucia mountains on the other, this stretch of coast along Route 1 is surrounded by astounding cliff faces and hazy views of the picturesque coast.

Why should I go? Route 1 is often voted the best drive in America, and for good reason. The road covers one of the most treasured coasts in the world, since it is the United States' longest coastline that remains mostly undeveloped. It's revered by many and described as almost mythical.

Due to its popularity, the coastline is protected rather profoundly, to preserve its natural state and charm. The opportunity to see a vast coastline so cared for is becoming rare, so taking your chance to visit it now would be unforgettable.

What should I do? Knock yourself out on its spectacular beaches! Start with Pfeiffer Beach—located off the beaten track, this beach is the home of the Keyhole Rock, so named due to the arch formed in it over time, where the last glimmers of daylight gracefully shine through, reflecting off the waves. The beach also possesses purple sand, at the north end, from garnet rocks in the cliffs. Jade Cove is worth a visit too—you might just find a lump of jade that could make your fortune!

Completed in 1932, the famous Bixby Bridge is one of the highest bridges of its type in the world, at 259 feet (79 meters) over the bottom of a canyon. The views down to the ocean below are stunning and well worth the pit stop.

The Old Coast Road is the route that was used before the opening of Bixby Bridge. Up the road, you can get a fabulous view of the coastline and walk among redwood forests to relieve you from the heat. People run, cycle, or drive along the Old Coast Road to enjoy the variety of scenery it presents.

Surfing along the Big Sur coastline can be hazardous, so make sure you look into weather conditions and the types of waves you'll experience at all the different beaches before you make your choice—lots of areas are safe for seasoned surfers only. Sand Dollar Beach is a good place for less experienced surfers to start.

Don't miss: McWay Falls is a breathtaking sight; the waterfall drops down the cliff on to the sand, flowing its way straight into the sapphire waters of the coast. You'll need to buy a ticket or kayak from another point over to the little cove it's nestled in to access the falls, but witnessing it up close is priceless.

Stand-Out Coast

RECIPES:
Beach BBQ Dishes

The burgers are sizzling away, the drinks are in the cooler and everyone's settling down for a chilled-out evening by the waves. Throw in one of these simple and delicious dishes to take your BBQ game to the next level.

Our memories of the ocean will linger on, long after our footprints in the sand are gone.

ANONYMOUS

GARLIC HASSELBACK POTATOES
SERVES 4

These individual, richly garlicky, oniony jacket potatoes are the perfect warm, filling side dish to your barbecued meat, fish, or veggie kebabs. Prepare them in advance and remember to put them on the grill first, as they will probably take the longest of all your BBQ recipes to cook.

*4 medium-sized
jacket potatoes
Butter or olive oil
Salt and pepper, to taste
8 garlic cloves
1 onion, thinly sliced*

Optional
*Cheese
Herbs, such as thyme,
rosemary or dill*

First, prick holes in the skins of each of your potatoes using a fork. Then cut 4 to 8 slits (depending on your skill and the size of the potato!) in the top of each potato, to about halfway down the potato.

Rub olive oil, salt, and pepper over the outsides of each potato and place on a piece of foil. Place a whole garlic clove in the slit closest to the center of the potato, and use an extra garlic clove per potato, thinly sliced, to fill the other slits.

Add a thin slice of onion to each slit, then add a drizzle of olive oil or a dab of butter to each.

Wrap the foil tightly around each potato and place at the bottom of your BBQ grill for 1 hour, or until soft.

Halloumi Kebabs
MAKES 4 KEBABS

250 g halloumi cheese, cut into chunks
1 red onion, cut into wedges
2 zucchini, cut into chunks
2 bell peppers, cut into chunks
8 cherry tomatoes
1 tbsp olive oil
Juice of half a lemon
Salt and black pepper, to taste

Put a cheesy twist on the classic BBQ veggie kebabs with lemony halloumi.

••

Wash and prepare the vegetables, and cut the halloumi into chunks. Thread the cheese and vegetables on to kebab skewers, alternating so you get at least two pieces of each ingredient per skewer.

Drizzle with olive oil and lemon juice, and season.

Grill on the BBQ for 5 minutes, or until the cheese is starting to brown and the vegetables are softening.

To me the sea is a continual miracle,
The fishes that swim—the rocks—the motion of
the waves—the ships, with men in them,
What stranger miracles are there?

WALT WHITMAN, "MIRACLES"

Sea Swimming

Whether you're lucky enough to live near the coast and regularly enjoy balmy waters, or your nearest spot for sea swimming means an icy dip with a full-length wetsuit quickly followed by a hot shower, there's nothing quite so therapeutic as simply slipping into the ocean's embrace and going for a swim. Swimming is not only great exercise (it's especially calorie-burning if in cold water)—it's also good for the mind and skin, as salty water is great for circulation, exfoliation, and extra-shiny hair.

For any wild swimmer, here is a bucket list of the world's best sea-swimming destinations to tick off:

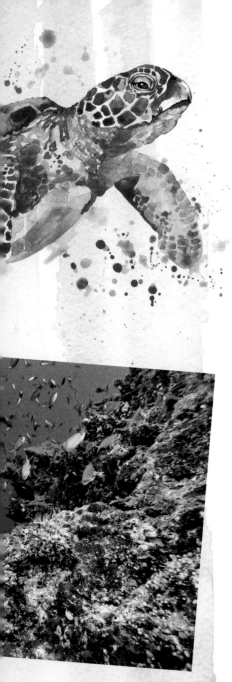

- *For the clearest water:* Linapacan Island, Palawan, Philippines
- *For the best city swim:* Valletta, Malta
- *For a swim in bioluminescent waters:* Mosquito Bay, Puerto Rico
- *For a swim in geothermally heated seawater:* Nauthólsvík geothermal beach, Reykjavík, Iceland
- *For a swim with spectacular coral-reef views:* Cayo Coco, Cuba
- *For a secluded paradise swim:* Dog Island, Panama
- *For a swim with a backdrop of Mayan ruins:* Tulum, Mexico
- *For a swim among 300-foot-tall (91-meter-tall) limestone-cliff islands:* Phi Phi Islands, Thailand
- *For a dip in Arctic waters:* Barrow, Alaska
- *For your best chance of swimming with turtles:* Hale O Honu ("Turtle Town"), Kauai, Hawaii
- *For a swim surrounded by colorful sea life:* The Maldives
- *For a swim among jellyfish, without getting stung:* Jellyfish Lake, Palau
- *For a swim with whale sharks:* Ningaloo Reef, Australia
- *For a swim surrounded by stingrays:* Stingray City, Grand Cayman, Cayman Islands

THE MYTHS AND LEGENDS OF THE OCEAN:
HERE BE DRAGONS

Picture the scene: a medieval cartographer hard at work on his latest Mappa Mundi (literally "clothes of the world"), filling in the lands and oceans that the grand, brave explorers of the wilds had thus far discovered. But what to put in the areas yet to be explored?

Monsters, usually. Any uncharted areas would be marked with dragons, sea monsters, basilisks, cynocephali, serpents, hippos, lions, scorpions, elephants, and even walruses, to warn of the type of creature believed or suspected to roam the region. They would usually be accompanied by phrases such as "here lions abound" or "in these places elephants are born," though the apocryphal favorite, "here be dragons," has only been found on two ancient maps, both made in the sixteenth century.

It's not hard to see why dragons and sea monsters held such fascination for these cartographers and ocean explorers—in its mind-boggling vastness and breathtaking variety of sea life, the ocean has been a source of wonder for centuries and has been the inspiration for thousands of myths and legends. Every coastal community seems to have its own stories and beliefs about the sea.

> So geographers, in Afric maps,
> With savage pictures fill their gaps,
> And o'er uninhabitable downs
> Place elephants for want of towns.

JONATHAN SWIFT

In Cardigan Bay, Wales, for instance, the sea god Dylan is believed to have called up an immense storm to steal away the three daughters of an old man. When he saw their father's obvious heartbreak, however, he repented and instead turned the daughters into seagulls so they could belong to both the land and the sea. So if you spot three white gulls on the Welsh coast, perhaps you're seeing the three lost daughters of Cardigan Bay.

In Australia, the ancestral Dreaming hero Ngurunderi is credited with creating many of the landscape features of the South Australia coast through his adventures. When he saw his two wives running to Kangaroo Island (which was then connected to the mainland) from Cape Jervis to flee from him, his anger was so great that he summoned the waters to rise, cutting off the island and drowning his wives, who became immortalized as the Pages Island rocks, which jut out of the Great Australian Bight to this day.

In one drop of water are found all the secrets of all the endless oceans.

KAHLIL GIBRAN

Some legends have their basis in some reality, such as in the case of "the Bloop." The Bloop is probably the most famous sound to have ever come out of the ocean—it was recorded in 1997 by the National Oceanic and Atmospheric Administration and captured the public imagination because it was too loud a noise to have been made by any known sea creature, though it sounds like marine animal sounds, and scientists couldn't determine its cause. Could it be the legendary kraken—part octopus, part squid (and possibly part crab or part whale, depending on who you talk to), all gigantic and all terrifying—out to destroy our boats and kill humans? Or could it be H. P. Lovecraft's fictional Cthulhu, a dragon–octopus hybrid so monstrous that simply looking at it can drive someone insane? Or perhaps it's the leviathan—the Bible's very own satanic sea monster, ready to eat up the damned after the Last Judgement? (The most likely explanation is that it was the sound of a large iceberg fracturing underwater, but let's not spoil everyone's fun.)

One of the most-feared myths of the sea is Davy Jones and his menacing locker. It's not known for sure where the legend originated and there's no unanimous agreement on whether Davy Jones was an evil, murderous pirate, the captain of a ghost ship, or the devil himself, but one thing is for sure: you don't want to end up in Davy Jones's Locker.

THE DOVER CLIFFS

Where? These magnificent cliffs rise up out of the English Channel on the south-east coast of England, looking out toward the French coastline.

Why should I go? To see England's natural beauty in all its glory, and amazing views of the English Channel.

What should I do? The best viewpoint from the high chalk cliffs is reached by following the coastal path toward South Foreland Lighthouse. Used for defense in both world wars, physical reminders of history remain, with slit trenches dug by soldiers in evidence along the cliff. You can also still see the remains of the range-finding station. Whistling Dame Vera Lynn's "The White Cliffs of Dover" as you go is optional. You can also take a boat tour out into the harbor to get the best views of the cliffs from the sea.

Stand-Out Coast

Don't miss: Walk the White Cliffs of Dover and you may be lucky enough to witness some unusual sights of nature as you stroll. The chalk grassland on the clifftop path is home to many rare plants and insects, including the pyramidal orchid and the chalkhill blue butterfly. Most often seen in bright sunshine, this little summer stunner has shimmering blue wings. When hunting for mates, the male butterflies can be found in their hundreds hovering just above the ground, forming a spectacular jewel-like carpet.

Exploring Tide Pools

Tide pools (also known as rock pools) are located in the intertidal zones on seafronts, and exist as separate bodies from the sea only at low tide. At high tide, they are subsumed back into the great oceans. They have long fascinated marine biologists with their unique ecosystems and the high adaptability shown by the few organisms that can live there—they must survive being exposed to the sun and wind, water loss, and wave action, not to mention exposure to predators when the tide is out. When they are revealed on the shore, they make for fascinating places to easily discover a wide array of special species. Here are some of the species that you may spot:

It is advisable to look from the tide pool to the stars and then back to the tide pool again.

JOHN STEINBECK

The best places to go rock-pooling:

- Roome Bay, Scotland
- Porth y Pwll, Wales
- Flamborough Head or Wembury Beach, England
- Fraser Island or Ricketts Point, Australia
- Treasure Cove Beach or Rockpile Beach, USA
- Chesterman Beach, Canada
- Discovery Bay, Hong Kong
- Ballito, South Africa

MUSSELS   STARFISH   SPONGES

ALGAE   SEA ANEMONES   SPIDER CRABS   CLAMS

BARNACLES   SHORE CRABS   SEA SLUGS

HERMIT CRABS   SEA PALMS   BLENNY FISH

LIMPETS   SEA URCHINS   ROCK GOBY FISH

SEAWEED   PERIWINKLES   LUMPSUCKERS

CUTTLEFISH   LONG-SPINED SEA SCORPIONS   SEA SORREL

SEA LETTUCE   NUDIBRANCH   WRACK

THE SANDPIPER

Across the lonely beach we flit,
One little sandpiper and I,
And fast I gather, bit by bit,
The scattered drift-wood, bleached and dry.
The wild waves reach their hands for it,
The wild wind raves, the tide runs high,
As up and down the beach we flit,
One little sandpiper and I.

Above our heads the sullen clouds
Scud, black and swift, across the sky:
Like silent ghosts in misty shrouds
Stand out the white light-houses high.
Almost as far as eye can reach
I see the close-reefed vessels fly,
As fast we flit along the beach,
One little sandpiper and I.

I watch him as he skims along,
Uttering his sweet and mournful cry;
He starts not at my fitful song,
Nor flash of fluttering drapery.
He has no thought of any wrong,
He scans me with a fearless eye;
Staunch friends are we, well tried and strong,
The little sandpiper and I.

Comrade, where wilt thou be to-night,
When the loosed storm breaks furiously?
My drift-wood fire will burn so bright!
To what warm shelter canst thou fly?
I do not fear for thee, though wroth
The tempest rushes through the sky;
For are we not God's children both,
Thou, little sandpiper, and I?

CELIA THAXTER

SEA LIFE: SPONGES, STARFISH, AND SEA URCHINS

Sponges

Though they look like plants, sea sponges are highly specialized marine animals that have existed for over 580 million years, meaning they are just about the world's oldest living creatures. There are 5,000 different species, varying in size from 1 inch to over 4 feet (from 2.5 centimeters to over 1.2 meters) long, and they often live in colonies (that can be formed as either sponge reefs or sponge ground), where their bodies provide shelter for small marine animals. It's not hard to see why they have often been thought of as sea plants, as they have no heads, arms, legs, muscles, nerves, organs, brains, ears, or eyes, and are incredibly simple multicellular organisms, but they are fascinating in their own right—and not just for their bright colors and variety of sizes, shapes, and textures. Having few predators (sea turtles and some fish) due to the toxins they produce, the fact that sponges do not move isn't too big an issue—instead they filter large quantities of water through the pores in their bodies to obtain food and oxygen and push out waste. If a sponge is cut (for harvesting by humans, for instance), it can regenerate and will often become larger and healthier than it was before, making them one of the most adaptable creatures in the sea. There's even one sponge in the waters off Hawaii that is 12 feet wide by 7 feet long (3.6 meters wide by 2 meters long) and is thought to be 2,000 years old.

Starfish

Starfish are not fish—they are echinoderms, a group of marine invertebrates known for their radial symmetry. There are around 2,000 different species of starfish, and they come in an array of colors and sizes. They live all around the world, even in polar regions, though most prefer tropical waters, and they can live for up to 35 years. Starfish usually have five arms, which they can regenerate either to regrow lost or damaged arms, or they can shed an arm at will if threatened by a predator. Their vital organs are mainly housed in their arms, so some species could regenerate the rest of their bodies from just a single arm and a bit of the central disc. It can take a year to entirely regrow an arm, though!

Sea Urchins

Sea urchins used to be called sea hedgehogs, because of their spherical shape and long, sharp spines. They are usually between 1 and 4 inches (3 and 10 centimeters) in diameter, although some species, such as the black sea urchin, have spines that can grow up to 12 inches (30 centimeters) long. They normally live for around 30 years but red sea urchins have been known to live to 200 years. Even when they're incredibly old, they do not show any classic signs of aging, with a 100-year-old urchin seemingly as healthy and capable of reproducing as a 10-year-old.

PROTECTING
OUR OCEANS:
OVERFISHING

While the oceans are a wonderfully rich and varied habitat, home to billions of fish, around 75 million tons (68 million tonnes) of fish are caught yearly—with only around 30 million tons (27 million tonnes) being for human consumption—and this number is rising rapidly. We eat more fish than cattle, sheep, and poultry, with fish and seafood being the biggest source of protein in the world, and the ocean is the primary source of food for more than 3.5 billion people. They may be rich in protein and the good fats, but if we continue to eat the same amount of the same species of fish, global demand will soon mean trouble. A "giant" cod in the nineteenth century was around 200 pounds (90 kilograms)—now, they rarely grow beyond 40 pounds (18 kilograms) due to overfishing. More than 70 percent of the world's major fisheries are being fished at levels beyond their sustainable limit.

> **THAT THE SEA IS ONE OF THE MOST BEAUTIFUL AND MAGNIFICENT SIGHTS IN NATURE, ALL ADMIT.**
>
> JOHN JOLY

So what can we do to help reduce the strain on these delicate ecosystems? Here are five ways you can immediately make a difference:

1. ***Eat less seafood.*** It may be a healthy source of protein, but if you can reduce your consumption of fish and seafood—even just having a few fish-free days per week—you'll be helping the oceans begin their journey to recovery.

2. ***Don't buy overfished species***, such as tuna, salmon, halibut, cod, swordfish, marlin, and especially shrimp. Populations of these species have been more than decimated—there are only around 10 percent of the number that existed ten years ago. Good fish to buy will vary depending on where you live, so check www.goodfishguide.org or the Greenpeace website to find out which species you should use as substitutes in your area. Generally, hake, trout, sea bass, mussels, and clams are safe bets.

3. ***Avoid buying fish caught by longline fishing***, gill nets, and trawl nets, which kill hundreds of thousands of seabirds and around 20 million tons (18 million tonnes) of by-catch (including small whales, dolphins, and porpoises) every single year. For every pound (0.45 kilograms) of fish you eat, 26 pounds (12 kilograms) of additional sea creatures are killed.

4. ***Buy local.*** Small fisheries are threatened by the super-commercial, huge industrial fisheries, and they're less likely to use trawl nets or longline methods, so support your local markets or vendors and buy species that live locally (and haven't been transported thousands of miles).

5. ***Spread the word.*** The more informed people are and the more people we have working together, the more we can do to save the oceans.

OCEAN CRAFTS:
Seashell Art

It is perhaps a more fortunate
destiny to have a taste for
collecting shells than to
be born a millionaire.

ROBERT LOUIS STEVENSON

Seashells come in such a stunning variety of shapes and colors that they lend themselves to all kinds of decoration—from the simplest glued-on-to-a-photo-frame project to jewelery and intricate art projects.

Simply making a small hole in your shells and threading them together can turn them into string curtains, mobiles, bracelets, or necklaces. Or use candle wax and a wick to turn bowl-shaped shells into pretty and unusual candles. Whether you paint the individual shells is up to you: try metallic paints on nicely shaped but dull shells, a sprinkling of glitter, or small colored dots of acrylic paint to create pretty patterns.

If you have a drill with a bit that's fine enough, you can try carefully and slowly drilling holes in your collected shells, but if you don't, here's how to make a hole in a shell without breaking it:

1. Decide where you want the hole to be, taking into account how you want the shell to hang. Bear in mind that the closer the hole is to the edge, the more likely it is to break. Go for the thickest area if possible, as it'll be the strongest part of the shell.

2. Use a pocketknife or pair of sharp nail scissors to scratch away a small part of the upper layer of the shell, around 1 mm deep.

3. Put the sharpest edge of the scissors or the point of your pocketknife against the scratched-away surface and twist it slowly against the shell, wearing through the layers until you reach the other side.

4. Continue twisting if you need the hole to be bigger. Otherwise simply blow or rinse away any debris and you're good to go!

Note: To clean your shells before use, soak them for 24 hours in a bucket with 1 cup of bleach for every 2 liters of water, then leave to dry fully (up to 3 days). You can also brush baby oil or varnish on the shells to bring out their colors and sheen.

THE SCOTTISH COAST

Where? Scotland is home to 10,250 miles (16,495 kilometers) of magnificent coastline, if you include the islands. The east coast is made of long beaches, estuaries, and nature reserves, while the west coast has fjord-like areas between lochs.

Why should I go? The variety of dramatic, brooding, treacherous but stunning coasts around Scotland is tremendous. There are craggy mountains, countless islands, fjords, and dazzling seas. You'll have continuously astonishing views and the added bonus of luscious nature thriving all around.

What should I do? Lunan Bay, along the Angus coastline in the east, is a particularly picturesque section of coast. It boasts 2 miles (3.2 kilometers) of pink sandstone hues, all overlooked by Red Castle, an old fortress full of history.

On the Isle of Staffa lies Fingal's Cave, made up of hexagonal columns of basalt, which appears very similar to the Giant's Causeway in Northern Ireland. Despite being uninhabited and only reachable by boat, it's an unusual sight to be treasured.

Or visit one of Scotland's many gorgeous, remote islands, for the chance of going hiking with absolutely no one else around and having entire rugged beaches all to yourself. Try Jura, Barra, Iona, or the loneliest island in the United Kingdom—St. Kilda, which was abandoned in the thirties when its small and aging population decided they could no longer support themselves. The ruins of the village are eerily beautiful.

You should also take the opportunity to go whale watching. The most commonly seen type of whale in Scotland is the minke whale, and on occasion orcas venture that way too. While a whale sighting isn't guaranteed year-round, if you plan your trip during the right time, you have a decent chance of spotting at least some dolphins and seals.

Don't miss: The west coast, where sea eagles (the fourth-largest eagle in the world) have returned after being wiped out during the Victorian era. The chance to see a resurgent

Stand-Out Coast

THE WELSH COAST

Where? The Wales Coast Path is a spectacular hiking trail which runs closely along most of the Welsh coastline. Wales is one of the first countries to provide a dedicated footpath right along the coast; it follows an 870-mile (1,400-kilometer) route between Chepstow in the south and Queensferry in the north.

Why should I go? To see Wales at its most beautiful, flaunting its beaches, estuaries, cliffs, and woodland areas, as well as its historical landmarks—and to see for yourself why Lonely Planet voted it the top region in the world in 2012.

What should I do? The entire route is accessible for walkers, with sections open to cyclists, horse riders, and wheelchair users, so take your pick! Pembrokeshire has long been lauded as one of the world's most phenomenal coastlines, but other areas are worth visiting too.

Stand-Out Coast

Take a walk down to Ynys Gybi, Anglesey, where an abundance of birds whoosh around the cliff and the sea's rock formations, while the sea crashes against the cliff face down below. There is an RSPB reserve in the area, so you can admire the varied species of seabirds, possibly even spotting a peregrine falcon.

Porthdinllaen is a quaint and picturesque fishing village, with access to the nearby Llŷn peninsula; a National Trust site that showcases the glorious mountain and seaside views, and is bursting with nature, especially down in its rock pools.

Don't miss: Visit Llanddwyn Island (which is not quite an island—it's connected to the mainland by a thin spit of land) for a romantic stroll in the summer or an exhilarating adventure in blustery weather. Scramble over rocky outcrops to explore the historic ruins on the island (they're what remain of a sixteenth-century church, which pilgrims used to visit to worship the holy well of St. Dwynwen, the Welsh patron saint of lovers), or sit back and enjoy an awe-inspiring sunset, looking out from the island.

KAYAKING AND SUPing

The calmer little brothers of surf-related sports, sea kayaking and SUPing (stand-up paddleboarding) have both been around for centuries, but in the case of SUPing, the sport didn't take off until recently. It's not hard to see why these two sports have enjoyed such popularity—both involve being on the water, using your own strength to propel you, but don't usually involve vigorous exercise and don't require the same levels of balance, expertise, and specialist equipment as other surf sports do (if you stick to calmer waters). Anyone can hire a sea kayak or paddleboard and drift along a bay or rugged coastline to explore the world from the oceans. Here are some of our favorite places to enjoy these most tranquil and harmonious of sports:

- Dubrovnik, Croatia
- The Bay of Bengal, India
- Hạ Long Bay, Vietnam
- The Lake District, England
- Mawddach Estuary, Wales
- The Californian coast, USA
- Milford Sound, New Zealand
- Bora Bora or Moorea, Tahiti
- The Belize Barrier Reef (the world's second largest reef system)

So throw off the bowlines. Sail away from the safe harbor. Catch the trade winds in your sails. Explore. Dream. Discover.

H. JACKSON BROWN, JR.

Lighthouses

In ancient times, if people onshore wanted to alert or guide mariners, they would light fires along hills or clifftops. The higher up the fire, the greater the distance it could be seen from—a principle which led to the first lighthouses being built, originally as markers for the entrance to ports rather than to warn boats of dangerous tides or shallow or rocky seas. The oldest known and most famous lighthouse was the Pharos Lighthouse at Alexandria in Ancient Egypt, which was constructed by Ptolemy between 300 and 280 BCE and stood at more than 350 feet (110 meters). The oldest existing lighthouse is thought to be the Tower of Hercules at A Coruña in Spain, dating from the first century AD. When transatlantic commerce started to boom, lighthouse construction began in earnest, and there are now more than 18,000 lighthouses around the world. Today, the most powerful lighthouse optic can be seen from 25 miles (40 kilometers) out to sea, or even farther if the light is reflected by clouds.

TOP LIGHTHOUSES TO VISIT:

- **_Rubjerg Knude Lighthouse, Denmark:_** This lighthouse is unique because, though it was originally built 650 feet (200 meters) inland with no sand dunes nearby, it has now been almost completely swallowed up by the amassing dunes that have been created as the sea edges ever closer to the lighthouse, eroding the coast as it goes. The fight against the rising dunes was given up in 1968, and it's predicted the lighthouse will soon fall into the sea.

- **_Tourlitis Lighthouse, Greece:_** Rising out of the sea on a jagged, eroded, and precarious-looking rock, the lighthouse you see today is a replica of the 1897 original, which was destroyed in World War Two.

- **_St. Nicholas Lighthouse/Church, Ukraine:_** This fantastically ornate chapel–lighthouse hybrid looking majestically over the Black Sea is dedicated to St. Nicholas, the patron saint of sailors.

- **_Eddystone Lighthouse, England:_** You can't visit the lighthouse itself without access to a helicopter to land on its helipad, but it's worth going to see for the spot's treacherous history—the lighthouse has had to be rebuilt three times, and the remains of an earlier incarnation can be seen from the shore.

- **_Jeddah Light, Saudi Arabia:_** The world's tallest lighthouse (at 436 feet or 133 meters) is also one of the world's most futuristic, looking a bit like a Christmas ornament skewered on a cocktail stick.

- **_Phare du Petit Minou, France:_** Set at the end of a striking, walled walkway (which looks particularly picturesque from the rocks down at sea level, where you can see the small bridge section near the lighthouse itself), this Brest lighthouse is over 150 years old.

- **_Yaquina Bay Lighthouse, Oregon, USA:_** A supposedly haunted lighthouse that was decommissioned for 120 years before being relit in 1996, it is now a museum and a rare case of a lighthouse sharing the same building as the living quarters.

SEA LIFE: WHALES AND DOLPHINS

WHALES

Whales are some of the loudest and most vocal animals in the world, with a variety of whistles, clicks, and other noises that can be heard by other whales in the water up to 15,500 miles (25,000 kilometers) away.

The blue whale is the largest animal that has ever lived: it's larger than the biggest dinosaurs, at over 100 feet (30 meters) long, and weighs up to 220 tons (200 tonnes). Its heart alone is the size of a small car, and its tongue can weigh the same amount as a full-grown elephant. They feed, however, on some of the tiniest animals in the ocean: krill. A blue whale can eat up to 79,400 pounds (36,000 kilograms) a day. They can swim at up to 30 miles per hour (48 kilometers per hour)! Newborn calves grow at an astonishing rate, putting on up to 210 pounds (95 kilograms) every single day up until the age of one year.

The sperm whale's head constitutes a third of its overall body length. Its brain weighs up to 20 pounds (9 kilograms), making it the heaviest brain of all living creatures. They sleep vertically, with the whole pod taking short, synchronized naps of up to half an hour at a time.

The gray whale has the longest migration of any mammal, at more than 10,000 miles (16,093 kilometers) per year, between Mexico and the Arctic.

And then of course there's the narwhal— the unicorn of the oceans. Its long, pointy tusk, which can grow up to 10 feet (3 meters), is actually an elongated and slightly bendy tooth. Theories abounded as to its purpose, from a weapon to something to attract the opposite sex, but it has recently been discovered that the tusk is used to stun fish and immobilize them, which makes them easier to catch.

DOLPHINS

Dolphins are well known for being one of the most intelligent animals on Earth, with Douglas Adams's brilliant line in *The Hitchhiker's Guide to the Galaxy* pointing out that while humans may think they're the most intelligent species because they created New York and the wheel, dolphins had just been mucking around in the water "having a good time," thinking *they* were the most intelligent species—"for precisely the same reasons."

· ·

When you think of dolphins, you're probably picturing the bottlenose type, but there are around 40 different species, including the largest species: the orca, or killer whale, which most people mistakenly believe to be a whale (we'll grant you that it's a pretty misleading name). Orcas are found in every corner of the globe and are the world's largest warm-blooded-animal hunter.

· ·

Dolphins usually live in pods of up to 12 members, although occasionally temporary "superpods" of up to 1,000 individuals can merge to take advantage of a particularly abundant source of food. Though they're popular in human culture, and thought of as elegant and playful creatures who have been known to come to the aid of humans, they are also brutal predators who hunt in packs with deadly efficiency. Dolphins breathe through their blowholes rather than through their mouths to prevent taking water into the lungs.

DOLPHINS SPEAK TO US OF THE RHYTHM OF OUR EMOTIONS: BREATHING IN JOY BEFORE PLUNGING INTO THE DEPTHS AND RUSHING TO THE SURFACE TO DO IT ALL OVER AGAIN.

ANONYMOUS

THE ARCTIC AND ANTARCTICA

Two of the last great wildernesses of our planet, their names inspire awe and make otherwise sane people want to go skiing, hiking, or even running across these humongous sheets of ice. Ten percent of the Earth's surface is covered in ice—mainly the gigantic Antarctic ice sheet. The Arctic in the north and the Antarctic in the south may seem similarly barren and icy, but in reality they're very different kettles of fish.

Antarctica facts

- Antarctica is technically a desert and is the world's biggest. It's also the world's coldest, driest, highest, and windiest continent.

- Its ice sheet has existed for over 40 million years.

- Temperatures can reach −135.8°F (−94.7°C).

- The ice sheet is an average of 1 mile (1.6 kilometers) thick.

- Antarctica has 90 percent of the world's fresh water.

- Some areas haven't seen precipitation for 2 million years.

- There are 7 churches in Antarctica.

- Antarctica is home to some notable animals, including penguins, albatrosses, petrels, seals, sea lions, and whales (such as killer whales and blue whales).

Arctic facts

- The Arctic refers to anything within the Arctic Circle (an imaginary line circling the top of the globe) and includes parts of Greenland, Iceland, Norway, Finland, Sweden, Russia, Canada, and the United States.

- It is home to around 4 million people—even though temperatures can reach as low as –94°F (–70°C)!

- The ice sheet at the uppermost part of the planet rests on water (not land), and averages 9 or 10 feet (around 3 meters) thick (although some areas are up to 65 feet [20 meters] thick!).

- Huge chunks of ice breaking off the Arctic ice sheet produce up to 50,000 icebergs every year, which slowly drift away from the pole and usually melt after about 4 years.

- The Arctic Ocean holds just 1 percent of the Earth's sea water, but the ice sheet holds 9 percent of the Earth's fresh water.

- The Arctic Ocean is the smallest ocean in the world, but still contains 25 times as much water as the world's lakes and rivers combined.

- Notable species living in the Arctic include: polar bears, walruses, narwhals, beluga whales, Arctic foxes, Arctic hares, and seals.

Stand-Out Coast

RIO DE JANEIRO

Where? One of the biggest cities in South America, Rio is perched on the southeast coast of Brazil.

Why should I go? Not just to party at the carnival or relax on the world-famous Copacabana and Ipanema beaches (though those things should be enjoyed in their own right at least once in a lifetime)—Rio has so much more to offer. Whether it's hiking up the imposing Corcovado Mountain through dense jungle to reach the Christ the Redeemer monument and drink in the awe-inspiring views, or taking the cable car to the top of Pão de Açúcar (Sugarloaf Mountain), there are breathtaking vistas galore from just about everywhere in this remarkable city.

What should I do? Rio is an active traveler's playground, with opportunities for all kinds of water sports on its many beaches and a glorious city to explore on foot. If hiking is your thing, check out the variety of trails on offer, from easy-going paths that skirt the coast to climbing up monolithic mountains (try the winding, wooded Cláudio Coutinho Trail for the chance to spot monkeys and lizards, and to get you to the base of Sugarloaf Mountain). Or you could try paragliding, floating in blissful quietude above it all.

Don't miss: Once you've exhausted yourself from one too many caipirinhas in Copacabana, head on down to Rio's lesser-known and more unspoiled beaches at Grumari (for a wild nature reserve, a surfing paradise, and a break from beachfront commerce), and Prainha (for lush rainforest-covered hills that plunge into the ocean, another surfing paradise, and phenomenal sunset views—Rio's coastline just looks even better at night).

How inappropriate to call
this planet Earth when it
is clearly Ocean.

ARTHUR C. CLARKE

COASTEERING

Coasteering is the art of traversing rocky coastlines by a combination of swimming, scrambling, climbing, jumping, and diving. Special shoes and gloves can be worn for extra grip and for protection from the rocks, and a wetsuit is usually worn—especially in the United Kingdom's chilly waters, where the sport originated. Of course, people have been scrambling over rocks and swimming across sections of sea to get to remote coves for centuries, but it only evolved into a guided recreational activity in the 1990s, on the Pembrokeshire Coast. The United Kingdom is still the home of coasteering, and the most dramatic sections of coast to take part in the sport are around the Cornish peninsula, the Northern Irish coast, Oban in Scotland, and Dorset's Jurassic Coast.

Beach Activities

No matter your age, a trip to the beach isn't complete without a few silly moments—skimming stones over the water, flying a kite, or building an elaborate sandcastle only to watch it wash away; all these take us back to being a child again, enjoying the simple pleasures that frolicking by the sea can bring.

According to sandcastle experts, the perfect sand for creating magnificent sand sculptures is found on Weymouth Beach, Dorset. The grain formulation and the consistency of the sand mean that you can try your hand at something more complex than your standard plastic-bucket affair. Just try not to get too competitive—castles in the sand never last for long.

To check out the work of some seriously talented sand sculptors, why not go along to one of the many sand sculpture festivals or competitions that take place every summer around the world?

There's Weston Sand Sculpture Festival in the United Kingdom, which sees a handful of gigantic sand sculptures take pride of place on the beaches of Weston-super-Mare every year; Sand Safari in Queensland, Australia, which pits ten professional sculptors against each other and fills Surfers Paradise Beach with spectacular creations; the European Championship Sand Sculpture Festival in Zandvoort aan Zee, the Netherlands; and many dedicated sand sculpture events around the American coast.

But the mother of all sand sculpture exhibitions is Sand City in Pêra, Portugal, which has hosted the FIESA International Sand Sculpture Festival every year since 2003. It uses 35,000 tons (31,800 tonnes) of sand to create 50 sculptures that are lit up on the beach in the evenings.

SHIPWRECKS

There are more historical artifacts—including an estimated three million shipwrecks—lying on the floor of the ocean than in the world's museums combined. Before the days of satellite navigation and accurate sea charts, shipwrecks were sadly commonplace due to the rocky reefs or sandbanks near many coasts lying undetected, just beneath the surface. These wrecks provide perfect homes for marine creatures, but they also give us a fascinating glimpse into bygone eras.

Famous wrecks, such as the *Titanic* and the *Mary Rose*, have captured the public imagination, but other wrecks are noteworthy for what has been found on board. For instance, the Dutch trading ship *Geldermalsen*, which sank in 1751, was carrying gold and porcelain, though its most valuable cargo at the time was its shipment of tea. Wrecks have been discovered of ships carrying gold (the value of the gold found so far aboard the sunken paddle steamer *Central America* exceeds $74 million), beautifully crafted and incredibly valuable Ming-dynasty ceramics, and in the case of a shipwreck off the Finnish coast, 168 intact bottles of champagne that had been slowly aging at the bottom of the sea for 170 years. The Baltic Sea's cold, airless water is

particularly good for preserving shipwrecks: the Swedish warship *Vasa*, which sank in 1628, was raised in almost perfect condition, its intricate carvings and ornate decorations just as impressive today as they would have been in the seventeenth century.

One of the most fascinating places to go shipwreck-hunting is Namibia's famed Skeleton Coast, also known, ominously, as "the Gates of Hell" or "the land God made in anger." This strip of coast is so treacherous because of an unfortunate combination of fierce trade winds and thick ocean fogs that batter the coastline for much of the year, the inhospitable desert and ever-shifting sand dunes that line the shore, and the prevalence of offshore rocks easily hidden in the fog, ready to catch the hulls of boats hurled at them by the unrelenting winds and cast them aside. Though the huge, bleached whalebone carcasses that once littered the shore at the peak of the whaling industry gave it its name, today it's the skeletons of over a thousand ships beached along the coastline that tourists come to see. The wrecks of ships of all shapes and sizes can be found every few miles along the coast, the most famous of which is the *Dunedin Star*. The cargo liner was transporting ammunition and supplies to support the Allied Forces in the Middle East, via Egypt, when she ran aground. A bomber and tugboat sent to their aid were also lost at sea, though, miraculously, other than two tugboat crew who were killed in rescue attempts, all the other crew, gunners, and passengers were rescued. The wrecks of the tug and bomber, as well as of the *Dunedin Star* itself, are all visible today.

THE SECRET OF THE SEA

Ah! what pleasant visions haunt me
As I gaze upon the sea!
All the old romantic legends,
All my dreams, come back to me.

Sails of silk and ropes of sandal,
Such as gleam in ancient lore;
And the singing of the sailors,
And the answer from the shore!

Most of all, the Spanish ballad
Haunts me oft, and tarries long,
Of the noble Count Arnaldos
And the sailor's mystic song.

Like the long waves on a sea-beach,
Where the sand as silver shines,
With a soft, monotonous cadence,
Flow its unrhymed lyric lines;—

Telling how the Count Arnaldos,
With his hawk upon his hand,
Saw a fair and stately galley,
Steering onward to the land;—

How he heard the ancient helmsman
Chant a song so wild and clear,
That the sailing sea-bird slowly
Poised upon the mast to hear,

Till his soul was full of longing,
And he cried, with impulse strong,—
'Helmsman! for the love of heaven,
Teach me, too, that wondrous song!'

'Wouldst thou,'—so the helmsman answered,
'Learn the secret of the sea?
Only those who brave its dangers
Comprehend its mystery!'

In each sail that skims the horizon,
In each landward-blowing breeze,
I behold that stately galley,
Hear those mournful melodies;

Till my soul is full of longing
For the secret of the sea,
And the heart of the great ocean
Sends a thrilling pulse through me.

HENRY WADSWORTH LONGFELLOW

SEA LIFE: SHARKS

Sharks may well be the most feared animal on the planet, but there are over 400 species of shark, and only a handful which pose a threat to humans (mostly the great white, tiger shark, and bull shark). It's not hard to see why they can be terrifying, though—whether it's their huge size and dead-looking, glassy eyes, or the fact that most sharks have around 45 gigantic teeth in their mouth in up to 7 fearsome rows (they grow teeth very quickly to replace lost teeth, and most sharks will get through 30,000 teeth in their lifetime). However, only around 10 to 30 humans are killed by sharks per year (compare this to the fact that around 50 people die every year falling from ladders, or that 30 people die by accidental drowning in the bath), while a shocking 100 million sharks are killed by humans in return every year. Here are some facts about these magnificent creatures:

HE WHO LETS THE SEA LULL HIM INTO A SENSE OF SECURITY IS IN VERY GRAVE DANGER.

HAMMOND INNES

Hammerhead sharks are one of the only animals that tan from the sun like humans do. These sharks are much more social than most species, living and hunting in schools of up to 100 other sharks. They give birth to live young—sometimes up to 50 live pups in a litter!

The largest fish in the ocean is the whale shark, which can reach lengths of 32 feet (10 meters).

Some odd things have been found inside the stomachs of sharks: a chair, an unopened bottle of wine, a drum, the rear half of a horse, shoes, a license plate, and even a tire.

There's a patch in the Pacific Ocean known as the White Shark Cafe, where hundreds of great white sharks congregate—even though there's hardly any food there. Researchers are still trying to identify the reasons for this odd behavior.

Sharks don't have any bones in their bodies—their skeletons are made of cartilage.

Though they're the second-largest fish in the ocean (after the whale shark), basking sharks feed on some of the tiniest animals in the sea—plankton. They swim with their 3-foot-wide (1-meter-wide) mouths open to filter over 1,800 tons (1,630 tonnes) of water per hour.

The cookiecutter shark feeds by attaching its mouth to its prey (often much larger fish, such as tuna and great white sharks, plus dolphins and whales) by suction, then spinning its body so its serrated teeth cut through the flesh, taking out conical chunks of meat.

Some female sharks can reproduce via parthenogenesis, which is essentially "virgin birth"—creating offspring without any input from a male.

Swell sharks are biofluorescent, shining bright green in the depths of the ocean. It's believed that the unique patterns of their biofluorescent markings are used for identification or for attracting a mate.

The oldest fish in the ocean is the frilled shark, which has lived nearly unchanged in the ocean for 150 million years, surviving 5 mass-extinction events. It has 300 teeth in 25 rows.

It's speculated that Greenland sharks can live for 400 years and don't reach sexual maturity until they're 150 years old. They're the longest-living vertebrates in the world.

RECIPES:
Seaside Drinks

If you're making these drinks at home, they'll travel fine in a regular resealable bottle, but why not take them in individual sealable jars or in a pitcher with a lid. Just remember to pack some ice cubes in the cooler!

MINT ICED TEA
MAKES 1 PITCHER

Per pitcher:

*3 teabags (green or
black tea works well)*
50 g sugar
1 lemon
Handful of fresh mint leaves

Brew three cups' worth of tea, and leave to steep for 10 minutes. Slice the lemon and add to the mix, along with the sugar. Swirl the mint leaves around to stir, then drop the mint leaves in. When cool, refrigerate until chilled, letting the mint infuse the tea. When ready to serve, strain the mint and pour over ice cubes.

Blackberry Mojito

This fruity twist on a refreshing classic will perk up any beachy party. You can premix the drink before you go, but it will taste so much fresher if you mix the cocktails in the salty sea air.

••

Cut the lime into quarters and place at the bottom of a tumbler or cocktail glass. Add the mint, sugar, and blackberry puree and muddle, then add the rum and ice cubes and stir well. Top up with elderflower cordial and garnish with fresh blackberries.

Per person:

1 lime
Handful of fresh mint leaves
2 tsp sugar
10 ml blackberry puree
60 ml white rum
Elderflower cordial
Handful of fresh blackberries

Flavored Ice Cubes

These flavorsome ice cubes will add fun and color to your drinks. Add them to plain water to give it a fruity boost, or try them in sparkling water, elderflower cordial, or iced tea for an extra kick.

Cut your fruit, veg, or flowers of choice into slices or smaller-than-an-ice-cube chunks. Place them in your ice-cube tray, top with cold water, and place in the freezer the day before your seaside trip—voila!

Here are some delicious combinations to get you started:

CUCUMBER AND MINT STRAWBERRY AND BASIL
GRAPEFRUIT AND VANILLA LAVENDER AND ORANGE
WATERMELON AND STAR ANISE GINGER AND LIME
BLUEBERRY AND ROSEMARY **LEMON AND LIME**

Decadent Hot Chocolate

Per person:
250 ml milk (full fat or a
dairy-free alternative)
50 g sugar
1 tsp vanilla extract
50 g dark chocolate, grated
(or 30 g cocoa powder)

For those cooler evenings after the sun has set, what better way to warm yourself up than with a luxuriously over-the-top hot chocolate?

....

Slowly bring the milk just to boiling in a pan over a camping stove then reduce the heat. Add the sugar, vanilla extract, and chocolate or cocoa powder and stir over the heat until combined. Taste and adjust according to your personal preference—more sugar if you have a sweet tooth, or more cocoa powder for a richer, thicker drink.

Why not try adding marshmallows, a tablespoon of heavy cream or condensed milk, crushed Oreo cookies, peanut butter, a pinch of cinnamon or chili, or even salted caramel sauce, and topping with whipped cream to make your seaside treat even more delicious?

After a visit to the beach, it's hard to believe that we live in a material world.

PAM SHAW

THE DEPTHS OF THE OCEAN

Descending from the sunlit surface of the water to the ocean floor, as the light fades to permanent darkness, the changes in the make-up of the ocean are drastic. Sunlight affects everything in the delicate ecosystem of the ocean, from visibility and temperature to the availability of food and amount of oxygen.

When you finally see what goes on underwater, you realize that you've been missing the whole point of the ocean.

DAVE BARRY

The first 200 meters below the surface are referred to as the "sunlight zone." There's enough light to support plankton, which in turn provide food for the majority of the marine animals we know about, including dolphins, sharks, most fish, and whales.

The next zone down, between 200 and 1,000 meters, is called the "twilight zone" (or, technically, the "mesopelagic zone"), because although the sunlight doesn't penetrate this far, there's still a faint blue glow of light filtering through. This zone is home to specially adapted creatures who can survive without sunlight, in colder waters, and with less oxygen—such as vampire squid, anglerfish, lanternfish, and other odd-lookers.

Past 1,000 meters, there's no light whatsoever, meaning that anything below this depth lives in total darkness (except for the light emitted by some bizarre animals in this region). The average ocean depth is 4,000 meters, which means a lot of deep, dark waters! Creatures living in this eerie zone (known as the "bathyal zone") include deep-sea squid, viperfish, whales, and octopuses, but there are no known plants at this depth. Animals living in the dark don't need to be as quick or strong, as their predators cannot see them, so most animals in this zone have soft bodies and weak muscles and often don't have eyes. Most creatures living here are small, to preserve energy, but the giant squid can grow to 43 feet (13 meters) long!

The deepest parts of the ocean (between 4,000 and 6,000 meters below the water surface) are known as the "abyssal zone." It lies in perpetual darkness, with icy waters, colossal water pressure, and barely any nutrients. However, there is still life here—though very highly adapted to cope with the extremes of the habitat. There are giant tube worms that live in hydrothermal vents, giant squid, dumbo octopuses, cookiecutter sharks, and anglerfish. Most animals at this

SEA GLASS

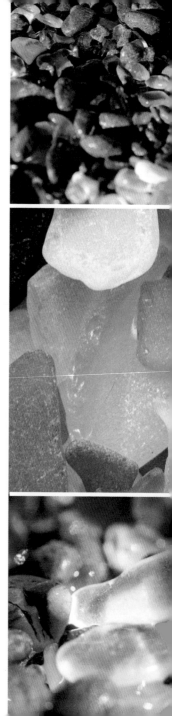

Sea glass comes in an array of beautiful colors, depending on the type of glass it originated from, years—sometimes decades or even centuries—before it wound up on your beach. Whether it was a soda bottle, wine bottle, beer bottle, medicine bottle, food container, or decorative glass item, it's now a beautiful piece of smooth, frosted glass with a long history in the sea. According to one old legend, "lucky" sea glass is gathered and used as bricks by sea fairies to build their palaces. Harder to find than ever before, the best hunting spot for lucky glass is on the fringes of shingle beaches. Should you find some, it is said that you should make a wish or pass the piece on to anyone in need of good fortune.

The most common colors are clear (from clear glass, turned white), brown, and green, while the rarer colors are accompanied by interesting tales. The pale aqua "sea foam" pieces nearly all come from the early 1900s—the color was popular at the time for water bottles, fruit jars, and ink bottles. Amber sea glass can date back to the late 1800s, when it was used for Mason jars, medicine jars, and snuff jars. You can even find lavender-colored sea glass, which would have been clear originally but, due to the manganese used in de-colorizing glass in the 1820s, the sun has gradually bleached the glass purple. The rarest colors— often from decorative glassware, stained glass, and even brake lights—are red, orange, turquoise, yellow, and black (which is often mistaken for a regular rock).

One cannot collect all the beautiful shells on the beach. One can collect only a few, and they are more beautiful if they are few.

ANNE MORROW LINDBERGH

From
"WITH A NANTUCKET SHELL"

I send thee a shell from the ocean-beach;

But listen thou well, for my shell hath speech.

Hold to thine ear,

And plain thou'lt hear

Tales of ships

That were lost in the rips.

CHARLES HENRY WEBB

Scuba Diving

Scuba diving is an incredible, otherworldly experience: not only does it let us see first-hand the splendors of coral reefs, sea creatures, and formidable sharks; it also lets us explore shipwrecks and—more recently—underwater sculpture parks. Whatever your dream dive site, here are our top picks to put on your scuba bucket list:

> From birth, man carries the weight of gravity on his shoulders. He is bolted to Earth. But man has only to sink beneath the surface and he is free.
>
> JACQUES COUSTEAU

- **Sistema Sac Actun, Yucatán, Mexico:** The longest surveyed underwater cave system in the world. While you're in Mexico, make a trip to the **Cancún Underwater Museum**, where over 500 sculptures have been sunk and pieces of damaged coral from the nearby reef have been planted to form a new reef—it's one of the largest artificial reefs in the world.

- **Yonaguni Monument, Yaeyama Islands, Japan:** Though it's tough to get to and can only be accessed by experienced divers, it's worth viewing this 8,000-year-old, smooth-stepped pyramid submerged under the sea. How it got there has puzzled experts for years, with some claiming it to be a geological phenomenon, some believing it to be the ruins of a long-lost city, and some even suggesting it was the work of aliens.

- **Kwajalein, Marshall Islands (Pacific Ocean):** Whereas planes and tanks have been intentionally sunk to create artificial reefs and dive sites elsewhere, this one is the real deal: after World War Two, all Japanese military evidence was scuttled in the waters around the islands. There are planes, cars, boats, and cargo to be seen, but they can only be explored with a guide due to the presence of live ammunition!

- **Banua Wuhu, Sulawesi, Indonesia:** Just 16 feet (5 meters) below the surface off the coast of Sulawesi, you'll find the crater of an active volcano. Its sides extend 1,300 feet (400 meters) below sea level, where coral reefs, reef sharks, barracuda, parrotfish, clownfish, and neon fusiliers thrive, making the landscape look like something from another planet. While the volcano last erupted in 1968 and may well erupt again, there's no danger from lava flows or toxic air, as the sulphur is released instead as a gas in a string of warm, silvery bubbles.

- **Aqaba, Jordan:** Explore extensive Japanese-garden-style coral reefs and colorful sea life, as well as the *Cedar Pride* shipwreck and an M42 anti-aircraft tank perched casually on the sea floor.

- **Christ of the Abyss, Portofino, Italy:** Dive down for a submerged bronze statue of Jesus himself—at 8 feet (2.5 meters) tall, he's pretty impressive up close.

- **Dean's Blue Hole, Long Island, Bahamas:** The world's second-deepest saltwater blue hole, at 663 feet (202 meters) deep.

HẠ LONG BAY

Where? You'll find this UNESCO World Heritage Site in northeastern Vietnam.

Why should I go? Because no other bay is quite so dramatic nor so unusual. With its 2,000 limestone islets and thousands of karsts around the bay, you can paddle around Hạ Long's emerald waters surrounded by towering limestone pillars topped with evergreen forests and explore hundreds of mystical grottoes.

What should I do? Explore! Whether by kayak, rowboat, sailboat, seaplane, swimming, diving, or snorkeling, you'll never run out of new caves or waterfalls to find or rocky outcrops to discover. You can also go climbing on many of the islets, and visit one of the four floating fishing villages that around 1,600 people call home.

Don't miss: There are several restaurants around the bay that offer the opportunity to have a cozy dinner inside a fairy-tale-like grotto, lit up with lanterns and candles, some of which offer glorious sunset views over the bay's unique horizon.

Stand-Out Coast

SEA LIFE: JELLYFISH, SQUIDS AND OCTOPUSES

JELLYFISH

Jellyfish may have existed in their current form for as long as 700 million years, making them the oldest multiorgan animal on the planet. They are found in every corner of the ocean—pretty impressive for creatures without brains. They come in all shapes and colors, and several species have some pretty bizarre "special features":

- A jellyfish goes through several complex stages of life, usually from a fertilized egg to a larval planula, to a polyp, to a free-swimming ephyra and finally a medusa. Some jellyfish will clone themselves at the polyp stage, and at least one species (*Turritopsis dohrnii*) is biologically immortal because, when at the adult "medusae" stage, if stressed, under attack, or suffering from disease, it can voluntarily revert back to the polyp stage and effectively start again.

- The box jellyfish has about 5,000 stinging cells in each of its tentacles and is the most venomous species on Earth.

- Some jellyfish are bioluminescent, meaning they can light themselves even in the darkest depths of the ocean. Certain species are known to use this skill when under attack, to attract an even larger carnivore, such as a giant squid or whale, to scare off (or gobble up) its assailant.

OCTOPUSES

- Octopuses have suckers, but never sucker rings or hooks like squids. They're completely boneless and can maneuver through incredibly tight spaces, and, like squids, they have three hearts.

- There are around 300 different species of octopus, with an average lifespan of 1 to 2 years.

- Octopuses are one of the most intelligent animals in the world—they can escape from closed twist-top jars, move and use sea-floor items as tools or for shelter, hold and manipulate objects, take advantage of fishing boats' nets and crab or lobster traps to steal food, and have even been known to jump on board fishing boats to take their catch directly from the container.

- Octopuses and some squids can change the color of their entire body, even mimicking the shapes and patterns of underwater objects to completely camouflage themselves, in as little as three tenths of a second. They can also use their color-changing abilities to send messages to other cephalopods—the Caribbean reef squid can even send one message to a squid on its left and a separate message to a squid on its right.

- Newborn giant Pacific octopuses are no larger than a grain of rice but will have an armspan of 14 feet (4 meters) when fully grown.

SQUIDS

- Squids are the fastest invertebrates in the world, capable of swimming at up to 25 miles per hour (40 kilometers per hour).

- The giant squid is the largest invertebrate in the world in terms of length, at up to 43 feet (13 meters), and weighs up to a ton (900 kilograms), with Frisbee-sized eyes. Its only predator as an adult is the sperm whale.

- In terms of mass, the colossal squid is the largest known invertebrate, with some estimates putting its weight at 250 pounds (750 kilograms). It is wider but shorter than the giant squid, with eyes of up to 16 inches (40 centimeters) in diameter.

BIZARRE BEACHES

Long stretches of pristine white sand and turquoise waters are all very well for a relaxing beach escape, but when you're bored of your picture-perfect tropical beaches, try these more unusual ones on for size…

A beach is not only a sweep of sand, but shells of sea creatures, the sea glass, the seaweed, the incongruous objects washed up by the ocean.

HENRY GRUNWALD

The **glow-in-the-dark beaches** of the Maldives—bioluminescent crustaceans light up the wet sand in neon blue at night-time, creating a beach that looks like a starry night sky.

The Beach of the Cathedrals in Ribadeo, Spain—where the sea has carved a series of cathedral-style buttresses and archways out of rock.

The interlocking, perfectly hexagonal basalt columns of the **Giant's Causeway**, Northern Ireland—the different-height columns resemble a gigantic pipe organ or staircase.

The **"dragon eggs"** lining Koekohe Beach, New Zealand—bizarre-looking giant boulders left on the beach when the surrounding softer rock was worn away.

The **glass beach** of Fort Bragg, California—literally a beach made of crushed, colorful and smoothed-away glass.

The **shell beach** of Shark Bay, Australia—where cockle clams have proliferated and their shells have taken over the shore.

The **hidden beach** at Marieta, Mexico—which can only be reached by swimming through a tunnel.

The **black-sand beaches** of One'uli, Hawaii, or Jökulsárlón, Iceland. On the Icelandic beach, giant, glassy chunks of ice are set off against the volcanic sand to dramatic effect.

The **red beach** in Tianjin, China—where a red plant (*Suaeda salsa*) blooms along the shore during autumn.

The **pink-sand beach** in the Bahamas—so colored because of the mineral, coral, and plankton make-up of the beach.

The **many-colored sand cliffs** at Alum Bay on the Isle of Wight, England—with strata of oxidized iron causing the vertical shafts of multicolored sand.

The **green-sand beaches** of Papakōlea, Hawaii, or Kourou, French Guiana—caused by a mineral from lava which has cooled in the sea.

Beach Yoga and Beach Running

Okay, so we might not all have pristine, smooth-sand beaches on our doorstep to go barefoot running along, the cool splash of the gentle waves refreshing our feet and our souls, or white sands to take sunset yoga pictures against, but there's something about just being near the ocean that elevates regular running or yoga to another level. The gentle lapping waves, the sound of the water trickling back over the sand, the cawing of seabirds—all can help transform your exercise into a pure, meditative state.

In still moments by the sea, life seems large-drawn and simple. It is there we can see into ourselves.

ROLF EDBERG

When anxious, uneasy and bad thoughts come, I go to the sea, and the sea drowns them out with its great wide sounds, cleanses me with its noise, and imposes a rhythm upon everything in me that is bewildered and confused.

RAINER MARIA RILKE

SANTORINI

Where? This island sits in the southern Aegean Sea, 120 miles (193 kilometers) from mainland Greece.

Why should I go? To witness its jaw-droppingly beautiful sunsets, multicolored beaches, famous white buildings, azure-domed churches, and placid windmills, and to experience the wonderful nightlife.

What should I do? Walk along the edge of the caldera (the crater left by a huge volcanic eruption thousands of years ago)—aim for any one of the island's quaint towns and you can't go wrong; visit Akrotiri, the ruins of a Minoan city destroyed in the eruption; cruise to the islands of Palea Kameni for its hot springs and Nea Kameni for its crater.

Don't miss: Watching the sunset from Oia (or any Santorini seafront, for that matter), as the lights of the town slowly twinkle into life.

Stand-Out Coast

OCEAN CRAFTS: *Build Your Own Raft*

Whether you've been inspired by Thor Heyerdahl's classic *Kon-Tiki* expedition and have your sights set on crossing the Pacific, or you just fancy playing around on a hand-made raft at the beach, here are the basics for making your own sea-going vessel:

1. First, you need to collect your logs or sticks of bamboo. The size of your raft will naturally depend on how many logs you have and how big they are, but don't worry—even a tiny raft will float (you might just have to make do with floating a leaf out to sea, rather than yourself). You want to use deadwood as it will float better than green wood. Most types of wood will work, but avoid porous wood if possible. The sticks or logs should be straight and roughly equal in circumference.

2. If you want to reuse your raft, you should varnish the wood and leave to dry before putting it in the sea to avoid it soaking up too much water and rotting.

3. It's best to construct the raft on the beach near to the sea to avoid having to carry the finished product far (it will be very heavy!). Lay your logs down next to each other and tie one end of your rope around the end of the first log, securing with a reef knot. Then use the rope to bind the logs together, wrapping the rope around the end of each log several times and around the whole structure twice. Make sure to pull the rope tight at all times and tie knots where you feel it could do with extra strength.

4. Lay an extra log on top of the raft at each end, at right angles to the base logs, to strengthen the structure. Add one in the middle too if your raft is long. Wrap the rope around between the individual base logs and criss-cross for extra security.

5. Test the raft carefully first in shallow water to make sure it floats. If it struggles to stay buoyant, you could try adding flotation devices such as Styrofoam sheets or empty plastic barrels to the underside.

6. Find yourself a long stick to use as a paddle, and then head out to the horizon! (But don't go too far out if the water is rough, of course—safety first, people.)

From
"DOVER BEACH"

The sea is calm tonight.
The tide is full, the moon lies fair
Upon the straits; on the French coast the light
Gleams and is gone; the cliffs of England stand,
Glimmering and vast, out in the tranquil bay.
Come to the window, sweet is the night-air!
Only, from the long line of spray
Where the sea meets the moon-blanched land,
Listen! you hear the grating roar
Of pebbles which the waves draw back, and fling,
At their return, up the high strand,
Begin, and cease, and then again begin,
With tremulous cadence slow, and bring
The eternal note of sadness in.

MATTHEW ARNOLD

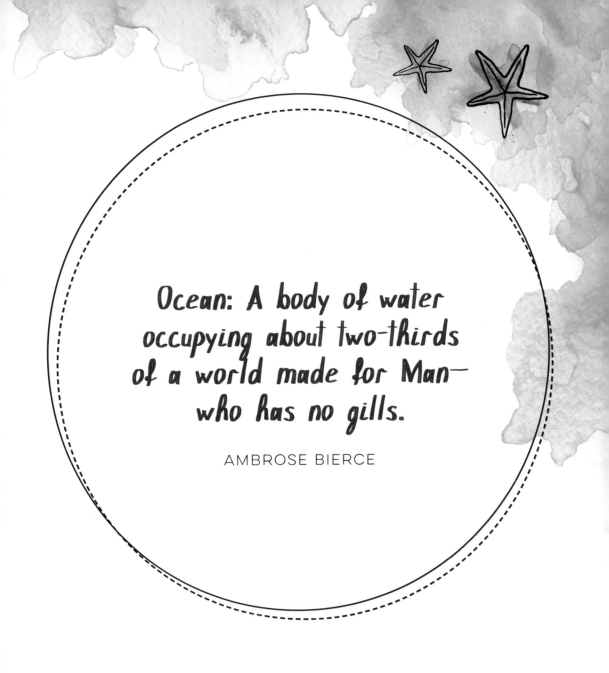

Ocean: A body of water occupying about two-thirds of a world made for Man—who has no gills.

AMBROSE BIERCE

> The world's finest wilderness lies beneath the waves.
>
> ROBERT WYLAND

SEA LIFE: SEAWEED AND KELP FORESTS

Seaweeds are algae, just like their little cousins, phytoplankton, so they're not true plants and nor are they animals—they're "protists" who can use the plant world's favorite trick for obtaining energy from the sun: photosynthesis. Their reliance on sunlight means they can only grow near the water surface, with some floating in the ocean while others are tethered to rocks on the shallow sea floor.

There are three distinct groups of seaweed: brown seaweed, which usually has large, thick, tough fronds; red seaweed, which is the type usually found on coral reefs and includes nori; and green seaweed, which includes species like sea lettuce.

Kelp is a type of brown seaweed that can grow extremely large and can form tall underwater forests which provide shelter (and sometimes food) for marine animals. From the tiny sea dragon, which looks like a floating bit of weed, right up to dolphins and sharks and sea otters, these forests provide a rich ecosystem for many marine creatures.

Giant kelp can grow up to 175 feet (53 meters) long and is the fastest-growing plant in the ocean, growing up to 3 feet (1 meter) a day. The sword-like blades of kelp have ball-shaped buoyant "bladders" that are filled with air and gas to help its blades stay upright, to get closer to the surface of the water and therefore access more sunlight.

THE ARCHIPELAGO SEA

Where? Finland is the easternmost of the Nordic countries, lying between Sweden and Russia, with a coastline on the Baltic Sea that is full of islands.

Why should I go? To see the world's biggest archipelago (a geographical chain of islands), to breathe the crisp, fresh, wintry air, and to experience the islander lifestyle in Finland's charming coastal towns.

What should I do? The best way to see the scope and complexity of the 50,000-island-strong archipelago is from the air, so helicopter tours are quite special in this area. However, if that's out of your budget, exploring the area from the sea itself is almost as good—whether it's a speedboat tour, hurtling around the archipelago with the sea air whipping through your hair, a more chilled-out boat tour to learn about the history of the various settlements and the verdant islands around the archipelago, or kayaking, to explore at will the bits that appeal to you most. There are national parks for those who like the great outdoors, ancient manors, fortresses, castles, churches, and lighthouses to delve into and picturesque wooden towns bustling with markets, cafes, artists' studios, quirky shops, and beautiful beaches to meander through.

Don't miss: Make a trip to the Åland Islands—an autonomous region of Finland with a rich and varied maritime history and 20,000 islands and islets simply teeming with beautiful, unspoiled landscapes, all, of course, within spitting distance of the Baltic Sea.

Stand-Out Coast

NORWAY'S FJORDS

Where? There are fjords all the way along Norway's winding coastline, but the most dazzling and iconic ones are found along the west coast.

Why should I go? For a relatively small country, Norway has one of the world's longest and most impressive coastlines, with 1,190 fjords, including two that have achieved UNESCO World Heritage status. Estimates vary (because the coastline has so many nooks and crannies and it depends whether you count the tiny islands and skerries), but it's at least 15,000 miles (24,140 kilometers) long, and possibly as long as 63,000 miles (101,388 kilometers), including all the fjord and island shores.

What should I do? With so many fjords to pick from, each one unique in its setting, size, and accompanying towns, attractions, and waterfalls, you could spend a year witnessing the sheer variety and beauty of them all and never get bored. The most famous are the Geirangerfjord (for all the rich greens and blues you could ever want from one panorama, plus some jaw-dropping waterfalls), the Sognefjord (the longest and deepest fjord), Nordfjord (home to the biggest glacier on mainland Europe), the Hardangerfjord (to see the Trolltunga "troll's tongue" cliff) and the Nærøyfjord (for unspoiled wilderness). Each one practically begs to be hiked, cycled, kayaked, or even skied.

Don't miss: Climb up to one of the many viewpoints early in the morning, and watch the sun rise over the fjord. Truly one of the most magical sights you'll ever see.

> I HOPE FOR YOUR HELP TO
> EXPLORE AND PROTECT
> THE WILD OCEAN... HEALTH
> TO THE OCEAN MEANS
> HEALTH FOR US.
>
> SYLVIA EARLE

PROTECTING OUR OCEANS:
PLASTIC, OIL, AND CLIMATE CHANGE

It is no exaggeration to say that if the ecosystems of the ocean collapse, human life will die out. We depend on the ocean not only for food, but also for oxygen—oceans provide up to 85 percent of the oxygen in the air we breathe. It's well documented that the oceans are under threat from global warming and human interference in the form of alteration or loss of coastal habitats, moving ballast water, and pollution. Consider these rather horrifying facts:

- Every year, humans dump more garbage in the sea than the total weight of fish they take from it.

- An estimated 1 million seabirds, 100,000 sea mammals, and untold numbers of fish die every year as a direct result of plastic waste in the sea. While their bodies decompose, the plastic does not, meaning it remains in the ocean to harm more creatures over and over again for thousands of years. Eight tons of plastic enter the oceans every single year—the equivalent of five shopping bags' worth of plastic for every foot of coastline around the world.

- On average, 600,000 barrels of oil per year are accidentally spilled from ships—60 percent of all oil consumed in the world is transported by oil tankers across the oceans. Add to this the oil that reaches the oceans as run-off from factories and cars on the roads (which is usually much more than the amount spilled accidentally), and that enters the sea as a result of offshore drilling, plus oil that naturally seeps into the ocean from the land, and the total amount of oil entering the sea each year is a scary 66 million gallons (300 million liters). Just 1 liter of oil can contaminate 9 million liters of drinking water.

- Changing water temperatures (as a result of global warming) affect plankton's ability to take up carbon dioxide and thus their ability to survive. As every living thing in the ocean depends on plankton for its survival, all organisms are threatened by each minor change.

- The average global sea level has risen by 5 to 10 inches (12–25 centimeters) in the last 100 years, and the rate is increasing. Island nations and low-lying countries are at risk of sinking into the ocean—Kiribati has already started to evacuate due to its rapid submergence.

WHAT CAN WE DO?

The single biggest and easiest thing you can do to help save the ocean is to reduce or cut out entirely all non-reusable plastics. Use reusable food containers, bags, straws, and water bottles, and avoid throwing plastic in the bin wherever possible. Refusing a straw in your drink and bringing your own reusable coffee cup when buying hot drinks or using a reusable water bottle instead of buying plastic ones will significantly reduce the demand for single-use plastics. You can even buy recyclable bamboo toothbrushes to avoid throwing more plastic in the bin every three months.

Pick up trash or litter at the beach whenever you visit and participate in "beach clean" events—and, of course, always take all your own litter home after a day at the seaside.

Never buy products containing microbeads—they are so small that they can't be extracted from the water at regular filtration plants, so they end up in the ocean, waiting for animals to eat them and be killed by their toxic plastic. Use natural exfoliators such as salt or sugar instead.

Use biodegradable cleaning products, especially for washing your car at home, to avoid washing grease, oil, transmission fluid, and antifreeze down drains which lead to the sea.

Quit smoking. Cigarette butts often end up in the sea, where they leach poisonous chemicals and plastics or get eaten by sea creatures.

Support organizations that are dedicated to cleaning up our beaches and oceans and campaign for policy changes and immediate action to save the ocean.

Spread the word. Most people don't realize the direct harm their everyday habits can have on the environment in general and the sea specifically, so educating others, making a stand against companies that have poor environmental practices, and contacting local representatives to encourage them to support marine conservation can all help.

For whatever we lose
(like a you or a me) it's always
ourselves we find in the sea.

E. E. CUMMINGS

WILD CAMPING AND BEACH BONFIRES

The fire is the main comfort of the camp, whether in summer
or winter, and is about as ample at one season as at another.
It is as well for cheerfulness as for warmth and dryness.

HENRY DAVID THOREAU

There are few better sensations in this world than falling asleep on the dunes, under
the stars, to the sound of the sea, and waking up with the sunrise, birdsong all around
(just check the tide tables to ensure you don't get a rude awakening in the middle of the
night!). Maybe the night before there were marshmallows toasting, someone playing
classic campfire tunes on a guitar, stories and drinks shared around the bonfire, warm
blankets and hot food. Camp-outs on the beach are one of life's simple pleasures
and can add a taste of adventure to the everyday.

TOP TIPS FOR WILD CAMPING ON BEACHES:

1. Find a spot that's flat, dry, and sheltered if possible, and away from footpaths—you don't want to be woken up by early-morning dog walkers! It also goes without saying that you shouldn't be camping on private land (especially near houses) without the landowner's permission—though if you follow these rules and pack up early in the morning, no one will even know you were there.

2. Check the regulations on your beach for lighting fires. If you do light one, be safe and ensure that you leave no trace of it when you go.

3. Take thermal layers, a warm sleeping bag, and a hat and gloves, even if it's summer—after the sun goes down, it can get rather chilly, especially next to the sea.

4. Don't forget a sleeping pad. Not only will it help smooth over all those knobbly, bumpy pebbles, but it keeps you off the cold ground, helping you keep warmer through the night.

5. If you need to do your business and there are no restrooms nearby, make sure you find a spot at least 160 feet (50 meters) from the sea and dig a hole for your "offering," which you can cover up again afterward.

6. Take a luxury item; something that will make your evening under the stars extra special—whether it's a big bar of chocolate, a hip flask with your favorite drink or some proper coffee to look forward to in the morning.

7. Remember the old saying "take only photographs, leave only footprints"? That still holds up today—be respectful of the land and take all your things with you when you go.

RECIPES:
Sunset Bonfire Desserts

The bigger you build the bonfire, the more darkness is revealed.

TERENCE McKENNA

TOFFEE APPLES SERVES 6

Toffee apples aren't just for Halloween—they also make a wonderful treat when the sun has set, the fire is roaring, and you fancy something sweet.

6 red-skinned apples
6 lollipop sticks
100 g sugar (demerara is best)
1 tbsp golden syrup
10 g butter

Optional toppings
Sesame seeds, crushed nuts, coconut flakes, sprinkles, chocolate flakes, melted chocolate or caramel

First, push a lollipop stick into the top of each apple. Next, put 25 ml of water in a pan over a low heat, add the sugar, and stir until dissolved. Add the syrup and butter and bring to the boil. Cook for 5 minutes, or until a drop of the mixture hardens when dropped into cold water. Dip each apple into the mixture, rolling to ensure it's completely covered. Lay out any toppings you've opted for on a baking tray and roll the hot, coated apple through the toppings—they should stick nicely. For chocolate- or caramel-covered apples, simply melt the topping in a bain-marie and roll the apple through.

Bonfire-baked Fruit

This is a simple recipe, and one which can be prepared in advance but cooked fresh on the beach over your bonfire.

....

Pick your fruit: bananas work well sliced down the middle, or wedges of apple, pear, peach, plum, apricot, or nectarine are great.

Place your sliced fruit on a large piece of foil, then sprinkle with brown sugar, vanilla extract, cinnamon powder, honey, crushed cookies or nuts, a drizzle of orange or lemon juice or a dab of butter—whatever flavors take your fancy!

Wrap the foil around the fruit and place on the coals of the bonfire for 10 minutes. Be careful retrieving your fruit—it'll be super-hot!

Serve with a dollop of whipped cream or ice cream for extra decadence (if you've brought a cooler with you).

S'mores

This American campfire classic is the perfect treat after a hard day swimming in the sea or a hard day's sunbathing—both are worth celebrating!

Marshmallows
Graham crackers
Toffee sauce
Chocolate

••

Roast your marshmallows on a stick over the bonfire until gooey and golden brown, and place on a graham cracker. Drizzle with toffee sauce, add a couple of pieces of chocolate, and top with another cracker to create a gooey, chocolatey delight.

SEA LIFE: MOLLUSKS AND CRUSTACEANS

Lobsters, shrimp, crayfish, and crabs all belong to the crustacean family, though there are 44,000 different species under this umbrella term, with nearly all of them living in the sea. They're protected by their hard exoskeletons, which they must molt whenever they outgrow them. They vary in size from the tiny 0.1-millimeter *Stygotantulus stocki* to the Japanese spider crab, which can grow up to 18 feet (5.5 meters) across from claw to claw.

There are almost 100,000 different species of mollusk, and it's the most varied phylum of any animal, ranging from octopuses and squids, to sea snails and slugs, to clams, oysters, cockles, mussels, and scallops. They don't have bones or exoskeletons but often have shells made of calcium. Here are some of the more bizarre features of the mollusk and crustacean world:

Clams are exceptionally long-lived creatures. The oldest known animal in the world was Ming, an ocean quahog clam, who was found to be 507 years old when he died (at the hands of the scientists who were trying to discover his age), meaning he was born before the first African slaves arrived in North America, before Henry VIII married his first wife, and before the construction of the Taj Mahal.

Male fiddler crabs have one oversized claw, which is used to intimidate predators, as well as in a kind of mating dance to impress females—this dance is where the name "fiddler" comes from.

Pistol shrimps have a secret weapon: their loudly snapping claw. This specialized claw snaps shut with one of the loudest noises in the entire ocean, which is loud enough to stun or even kill its victim outright.

Though all lobsters turn red when they're cooked, the chances of finding a live red lobster in the ocean are around one in ten million. Lobsters can be yellow, blue, orange, white, or mottled when alive—quite the colorful creature! They can regrow claws, legs, or other lost body parts.

Nautiluses have existed since before the dinosaurs—for around 500 million years. They're known for their large (up to 10 inches or 25 centimeters across), beautifully colored, stripy shells, but what's less known is that they can produce a thick slime to coat their shell as a form of defense, making them too slippery for predators to catch or bite into. They also have up to 90 arms, which are sticky to help them catch prey. They can live for up to 20 years, though their memory span is less than 24 hours. Pretty bizarre, I'd say.

THE TANG OF THE UNTAINTED,
FRESH, AND FREE SEA AIR WAS
LIKE A COOL, QUIETING THOUGHT.

HELEN KELLER

Beach Huts

The rows of cheerful, colorful huts that famously line the seafront at British beaches—and at Wimereux (France), Cape Town (South Africa), Port Phillip Bay (Australia) and Nesodden (Norway)—evolved from Victorian "bathing machines." These were wooden huts with wheels and usually two doors: one beach-side, for the user to enter in their street clothes; and one sea-side, for them to exit the hut straight into the sea, after having changed into their extremely modest bathing costumes and having rolled their machines into the sea. It was considered incredibly improper for anybody to be seen wearing bathing costumes out of the water.

Nowadays, luckily, the huts are much more likely to be used to store beach games and sports equipment, or as somewhere to sit out of the sunshine or wind. They're incredibly sought-after, often with long waiting lists to purchase one—in the United Kingdom prices can reach £35,000, while the most expensive beach hut ever sold went for $285,000 in Australia. The Queen even had her own beach hut in Norfolk until it was destroyed by fire in 2003.

THE GREAT OCEAN ROAD

Where? This 151-mile (243-kilometer) road follows the southeastern coast of Australia, in the state of Victoria, between Torquay and Allansford.

Why should I go? For the world-famous scenery—craggy, imposing limestone cliff faces, and rainforests—perfect surf and the chance to spot a koala bear up close and personal.

What should I do? This scenic route is just begging to be driven in a fancy car with the top down, taking in the dazzling landscapes and blaring out some tunes. Stop off at as many of the outstanding and unique viewpoints as you can along the way, including: the Twelve

Apostles, for eight (yes, only eight) towering stacks along the meandering coastline; London Arch (previously known as London Bridge, until one of the two arches in this flat-topped headland collapsed into the sea); the self-explanatory Bay of Islands; and Loch Ard Gorge, which is named after a ship which ran aground in the area and features two rock pillars (called Tom and Eva, after the two teenage survivors of the wreck). If you prefer two feet to four wheels, check out the adjacent Great Ocean Walk footpath. You can also take the opportunity to spot kangaroos, southern right whales, dolphins, platypuses, echidnas, emus, seals, and possibly even blue whales.

Don't miss: The Grotto—one of the only points along the coast where you can see the crashing waves from near sea level, rather than from the sheer cliffs.

Stand-Out Coast

I must go down to the
seas again, to the lonely
sea and the sky,
And all I ask is a tall ship
and a star to steer her by.

JOHN MASEFIELD

Conclusion

The sea is everything. It covers seven-tenths
of the terrestrial globe. Its breath is pure and
healthy. It is an immense desert, where man is never
lonely, for he feels life stirring on all sides.

JULES VERNE, *TWENTY THOUSAND
LEAGUES UNDER THE SEA*

More than two-thirds of our planet's surface is covered in water; the Earth's oceans are home to an abundance of sealife more varied, bizarre, and fascinating than even Jules Verne could have imagined—and we've still barely scratched the surface. With ever-improving technology and highly skilled researchers able to investigate deeper than ever before, it is almost certain that we will discover many more unusual and unimaginable species in the years to come.

It is now believed that the deep oceans could even be where the very first life on Earth came into being. Even though we walk on land, perhaps this explains why, again and again, we are drawn back to the enthralling, mysterious, incredible waters of the sea.

IMAGE CREDITS

p.1—top left photo (dolphin)—© Willyam Bradberry/Shutterstock.com; top right photo (waves)—© Pavel Vakhrushev/Shutterstock.com; middle right image (fish)—© vavavka/shutterstock.com; bottom left image (lighthouse)—© LAATA9/Shutterstock.com; bottom middle photo (shells)—© givaga/Shutterstock.com; rope pattern—© Irina Danyliuk/Shutterstock.com; p.3—background ©Jacob_09/shutterstock.com; p.4-5—background © Reconcept/shutterstock.com; p.8-9—background ©Jacob_09/shutterstock.com; p.5-6—background © Reconcept/shutterstock.com; p.11—background © Norrapat Teapnarin/shutterstock.com; p.12-13—fish © vavavka/shutterstock.com; photo © AlexZaitsev/shutterstock.com; p.14-15—wood texture © arigato/shutterstock.com; stones © Kriengsuk Prasroetsung/shutterstock.com; fossils © frantic00/shutterstock.com; p.16-17—watercolor © Norrapat Teapnarin/shutterstock.com; p.18-19 © eFesenko/shutterstock.com; p.20-21 © Titood99/shutterstock.com; p.23—top photo © margo_black/shutterstock.com; middle photo © Narcis Parfenti/shutterstock.com; bottom photo © divedog/shutterstock.com; p.24—top photo © Michaelpuche/shutterstock.com; middle photo © gallimaufry/shutterstock.com; bottom photo © timsimages/shutterstock.com; p.25—top photo © Tatiana Kilimnik/shutterstock.com; middle photo © Aristokrates/shutterstock.com; bottom photo © GOLFX/shutterstock.com; p.26-27—anchor © Christos Georghiou/shutterstock.com; boats © Anna Om/shutterstock.com; p.28-29 © Khoroshunova Olga/shutterstock.com; p.30-31—photo © its_al_dente/shutterstock.com; shrimp © maritime_m/shutterstock.com; p.32-33—photo © Yurchenko Iryna/shutterstock.com; fish © Pinchuk Oleksandra/shutterstock.com; p.34-35 © Michelle Schut/shutterstock.com; p.36-37—top photo © Joshua Raif/shutterstock.com; bottom left photo © Sergey Sidelnikov/shutterstock.com; bottom right photo © jo Crebbin/shutterstock.com; bird sketches © Anton V. Tokarev/shutterstock.com; p.38-39—top left photo © Natural Earth Imagery/shutterstock.com; top right photo © vladsilver/shutterstock.com; middle bottom photo © TravelMediaProductions/shutterstock.com; fish © vavavka/shutterstock.com; p.40-41—photo © Anna Om/shutterstock.com; p.42-43—background © Jacob_09/shutterstock.com; center photo © Igor Plotnikov/shutterstock.com; top right photo © Burben/shutterstock.com; p.44-45—background © Jacob_09/shutterstock.com; center photo © Artem Avetisyan/shutterstock.com; right-hand

com; bottom photo © Kokhanchikov/shutterstock.com; top right photo © Yellowj/shutterstock. com; p.86-87—wood texture © arigato/shutterstock.com; nets © Vasilyeva Larisa/shutterstock. com; p.88-89—top right photo © Stepan Zhukov/shutterstock.com; top left photo © aragami12345s/shutterstock.com; bottom left photo © PopTika/shutterstock.com; bottom right photo © Oleksandr Kavun/shutterstock.com; p.90-91 © Swen Stroop/shutterstock.com; p.92-93 © Mark Bridger/shutterstock.com; p.94-95 © danielcastromaia/shutterstock.com; p.96—left photo © Stephane Bidouze/shutterstock.com; right photo © Lemonakis Antonis/shutterstock. com; p.98-99—watercolor wash © Anastasiya Samolovova/shutterstock.com; left photo © Seb c›est bien/shutterstock.com; right photo © CO Leong/shutterstock.com; narwhale illustration © Kat_Branch/shutterstock.com; p.100-101 © First Step Studio/shutterstock.com; p.102-103—top left photo © vladsilver/shutterstock.com; middle photo © Wim Hoek/shutterstock.com; right photo © Fotokon/shutterstock.com; p.104-105 © SJ Travel Photo and Video/shutterstock.com; p.107—watercolor wash © Norrapat Teapnarin/shutterstock.com; top photo © Noppharat888/ shutterstock.com; bottom photo © Photobac/shutterstock.com; p.108-109 © Kharlanov Evgeny/shutterstock.com; p.110-111 © Richard Whitcombe/shutterstock.com; p.112-113—watercolor wash © Norrapat Teapnarin/shutterstock.com; p.114-115—bottom middle photo © Brandelet/shutterstock.com; right photo © Alexyz3d/shutterstock.com; p.116-117—left photo © Matt9122/shutterstock.com; right photo © Yoshinori/shutterstock.com; p.118-119 © Elena Veselova/shutterstock.com; p.120—left photo © Ekaterina Kondratova/shutterstock.com; right photo © Kostiantyn Kravchenko/shutterstock.com; p.121—left photo © 5 second Studio/ shutterstock.com; right photo © Maria Uspenskaya/shutterstock.com; p.122—left photo © Stephanie Frey/shutterstock.com; right photo © iravgustin/shutterstock.com; p.124—watercolor wash © Anastasiya Samolovova/shutterstock.com; squid © graphixmania/shutterstock.com; angler fish © SketchingG/shutterstock.com; dolphin © eva_mask/shutterstock.com; whale © harmonia_green/shutterstock.com; lantern fish © Aurelija Diliute/shutterstock.com; p.126-127—top left photo © ThanusakS/shutterstock.com; middle left photo © Cebas/shutterstock. com; top right photo © Raivis Pienkarts/shutterstock.com; bottom left photo © Wollertz/ shutterstock.com; bottom right photo © Kuttelvaserova Stuchelova/shutterstock.com; p.128-